PROTECTING CHILDREN
A social model

Brid Featherstone, Anna Gupta, Kate Morris
and Sue White

P

First published in Great Britain in 2018 by

Policy Press
University of Bristol
1-9 Old Park Hill
Bristol
BS2 8BB
UK
t: +44 (0)117 954 5940
pp-info@bristol.ac.uk
www.policypress.co.uk

North America office:
Policy Press
c/o The University of Chicago Press
1427 East 60th Street
Chicago, IL 60637, USA
t: +1 773 702 7700
f: +1 773-702-9756
sales@press.uchicago.edu
www.press.uchicago.edu

British Library Cataloguing in Publication Data
A catalogue record for this book is available from the British Library

Library of Congress Cataloging-in-Publication Data
A catalog record for this book has been requested

ISBN 978-1-4473-3275-6 paperback
ISBN 978-1-4473-3273-2 hardcover
ISBN 978-1-4473-3276-3 ePub
ISBN 978-1-4473-3277-0 Mobi
ISBN 978-1-4473-3274-9 ePdf

Cover design by Robin Hawes
Front cover image: www.alamy.com
Printed and bound in Great Britain by CMP, Poole
Policy Press uses environmentally responsible print partners

Acknowledgements

Many colleagues and friends have helped shape our ideas, too many to name, but all very much appreciated. Particular thanks to Bernie Jackson and Danny Conway who contributed specific practice reflections, but also all the practitioners who discussed and debated the ideas with us. Thanks also to Jo Warner for her work on the original article that helped start the work for this book. Finally, thanks to all our families for their ongoing support, and to Policy Press for their patience!

Contents

ONE

Introduction

In 2014 *Re-imagining Child Protection: Towards Humane Social Work with Families* (Featherstone, White and Morris, 2014) was published. It was greeted with great interest and there was an overwhelmingly positive response to the critical review it undertook of contemporary child protection and its plea for humane practice. It resonated with practitioners and policy makers alike and suggested simply doing more of the same was neither ethical nor practicable. The book concluded by arguing for change in order to create policies and practices that inspired hope.

Many would argue that the problems have become more, not less, acute in the intervening period and the anxieties about the future set out in *Re-imagining Child Protection* have become more fully realised in the context of continued austerity and its disproportionate focus and impact on deprived families and local authorities. However, there have been also been more hopeful developments, including new empirical work that increases our understandings, innovations in practice that push at the constraints of the existing child protection project and fresh alliances seeking change. Using these positive developments this book is concerned with moving the discussion forward, and with seeking to provoke conceptual and applied debates that might offer children and families a more hopeful future when they face problems, uncertainties and harm.

Telling a new story

George Monbiot (2017: 1) argues that '[y]ou cannot take away someone's story without giving them a new one. It is not enough to challenge an old narrative, however outdated and discredited it may be. Change happens only when you replace it with another.' In this book we tell a new story, but one that has familiar chapters, rooted in social work's history. It is informed by our ethical positions and our research, and is encouraged by our engagement with those who experience current systems, and those who work in them. Like all good stories, there is room in the telling for different voices to chip in, add, challenge and, indeed, revise. Thus, while we consider the book contains much of what is needed to get us started on the road to transformation, it is only the start. As we go along, we identify what needs to change, why and how, but we also highlight the allies and conversations needed for the next steps.

As the activist, Rebecca Solnit notes:

> Changing the story isn't enough in itself, but it has often been foundational to real changes. Making an injury visible and public is usually the first step in remedying it, and political change often follows culture, as what was long tolerated is seen to be intolerable, or what was overlooked becomes obvious. *Which means that every conflict is in part a battle over the story we tell, or who tells and who is heard.* (2016: xiv, our emphasis)

Thus, a crucial part of our project is to expand and legitimise opportunities for different types of dialogue, storytellers and audiences. In particular, we highlight the importance of dialogue between those who experience services and those who design them, and, crucially, between those, who do not see the importance of linking actions to protect children with those concerned to tackle inequalities and social isolation, and those who give the dynamic relations between the two a more central place.

Locating our story

Across many countries, including the UK, the settlement between the state and its citizens, forged post war, has been undermined, if not broken, by a variety of economic and social developments (Davies, 2017). Increasingly, citizens' expectations of decent work, secure and affordable housing, and enough to eat can no longer be guaranteed by a state that is experienced as both intrusive and neglectful, especially by the poor, with a subsequent loss of trust and widespread feelings of alienation and disconnection (Davies, 2017, Monbiot, 2017, Peston, 2017).

A key argument of this book is that the policies and practices that have been developed to protect children need to be understood and located within this wider canvas and, indeed, have come to exemplify a punitive and neglectful state in many respects. This is deeply distressing given the enormous amount of effort and good will extended by a very wide range of constituencies to keeping children safe and making systems work. But in this book we suggest it is vital that we interrogate the history of such efforts and their intimate intersection with wider social policies and social trends (see Parton, 1985, 1991). In this Introduction we offer a brief highlight but Chapters two and three provide a much more thorough engagement with past, present and, indeed if we continue on our present trajectory, future dangers and possibilities.

The modern child protection system emerged in the 1960s rooted in a concern to stop babies dying or being 'battered' by parents, who were considered to be suffering from a lack of empathic mothering in their own lives. Poverty, bad housing and other social factors were screened out as holding helpful explanatory value in relation to why some babies were seriously harmed by their carers (Parton, 1985). It was considered that the post-war welfare settlement provided for the basic needs (such as income, housing, health care and education) of the majority of citizens, but there were some who were damaged by earlier psychological experiences and needed therapeutic help to care safely.

Walkerdine and Lucey (1989) explored the social democratic context in which these perspectives were formed. They noted that a strong movement in the 1940s and 1950s tried to produce a possibility of social reform through the agency of the mother. After the horrors of World War 2, the pessimism of social Darwinism was countered by an environmentalism, which emphasised the possibility of social reform through love and nurturance.

From those beginnings, rooted in care for babies who were powerless and voiceless, and compassion for emotionally deprived parents, the system has expanded enormously in terms of remit, research base, influence and power within a complex and changing society. Indeed, in his comparison of the reports into the death of Maria Colwell in the early 1970s and that of Victoria Climbié 30 years later, Parton (2004) notes differences not only in how the reports themselves were constructed, but also in the following: globalisation and identity; expert knowledge; systematic care, responsibility and accountability; managerialisation; trust and uncertainty; and the legislative contexts. To this we would add the unravelling of core aspects and assumptions behind the welfare state and the emergence of a discourse around individual responsibility and risk that encompasses cause, consequence and attribution.

As Bauman (2007: 14) notes, '[a]lthough the risks and contradictions of life go on being as socially produced as ever, the duty and necessity of coping with them has been delegated to our individual selves'. This has had some pernicious and under-examined effects in child protection where the basic elements of a story honed in a very different climate to that of today have proved remarkably resilient. The investigation and monitoring of the actions or inactions of individual parents/carers and focus on the intra-familial as the locus of cause and consequences takes on quite a different complexion in a climate of responsibilisation rather than compassion.

The current child protection story goes something like this:

- The harms children and young people need protecting from are normally located within individual families and are caused by actions of omission or commission by parents and/or other adult caretakers.
- These actions/inactions are due to factors ranging from poor attachment patterns, dysfunctional family patterns, parenting capacity, faulty learning styles to poor/dangerous lifestyle choices.
- The assessment of risk and parenting capacity is 'core business' and interventions are focused on effecting change in family functioning.
- Developing procedures, expert risk assessment and multi-agency working are central to protecting children.

A growing evidence base is disrupting this story, requiring engagement with troubling issues. The evidence highlights that the families who are engaged by services are poor, but poverty is curiously invisible in practice and policy accounts. This can be seen as an instance of 'public blindness' termed by Haebich (2007: 21) as 'the twilight of knowing and not knowing', where discriminatory treatment becomes normalised to the extent that it is rendered unremarkable. In more recent years, however, this 'public blindness' has become harder to sustain and has led to paradoxical developments where there is increased agreement that continuing austerity and the associated deprivation is driving care demand and that services need more money, at the same time as an apparent reluctance to apply that logic to families themselves and understand the role played by poverty and associated issues in their difficulties.

While explanations for children's maltreatment are routinely seen through a gaze that focuses on what happens in the home, the brain, internal cognitions, learning patterns and family dynamics, the following trend has, until recently, gone unremarked: the inequalities in children's chances of being able to grow up in their families of origin and the systematic links with deprivation and children being looked after (see Figure 1, see also Bywaters et al, 2018).

Figure 1: CLA* not at home or with relatives or friends by Deprivation Quintile, UK Countries, 2015

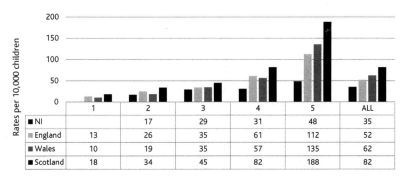

	1	2	3	4	5	ALL
■ NI		17	29	31	48	35
▦ England	13	26	35	61	112	52
▪ Wales	10	19	35	57	135	62
■ Scotland	18	34	45	82	188	82

Source: Briefing Paper 1, Child Welfare Inequalities Project.
* CLA refers to children looked after.

This relationship between deprivation and interventions obliges the asking of questions that are common in health and mental health, concerning the social determinants of particular behaviours and states of mind. Thus, for example, a World Health Organization-commissioned report on mental health (Friedli, 2009: iii) notes:

> Mental health is a fundamental element of the resilience, health assets, capabilities and positive adaptation that enable people both to cope with adversity and to reach their full potential and humanity. Mental health is also the key to understanding the impact of inequalities on health and other outcomes. It is abundantly clear that the chronic stress of struggling with material disadvantage is intensified to a very considerable degree by doing so in more unequal societies.

Because of the individualist focus in child protection, however, there are no mechanisms for understanding and engaging with the links between differing health and welfare outcomes in particular contexts. Because we lack knowledge about particular social and economic contexts, we are deprived of important understandings about the ecology of children's lives As we have illustrated above, there are very clear differences in looked after children (LAC) rates that are systematically linked to levels of deprivation. Thus, children in the most deprived areas are nearly ten times more likely to be removed according to the statistics above. But what is also important is that a town such as Blackpool, with high rates of children who are looked after, also reports England's lowest subjective happiness score and is the place where most anti-depressant prescriptions are written (Clark with Heath, 2014). Moreover, male life expectancy at birth in Blackpool is 74.7 by contrast with an affluent area such as Wokingham where it is 81.8 (ONS, 2016). Such data tells us that the opportunities to live well and love safely are not equally available to our children or their families. Moreover, as we explore further in Chapter five, the state's response in recent years has exacerbated such inequalities. As Webb and Bywaters (2018) note, almost all local authorities have faced cuts under austerity but the more deprived local authorities have faced much bigger average reductions. Between 2010/11 and 2016/17 the most deprived 20% of local authorities faced cuts of 27% in average population-weighted total children's services spend per child, after controlling for inflation. The least deprived 20% faced cuts of 4%.

The 'core abuse types' of physical abuse and sexual abuse, which once made up the bulk of child protection registrations in most parts of the UK, now account for only a minority of cases (Bunting et al, 2017). This mirrors trends internationally, with the majority of children subject to child protection registration/intervention in countries such as Australia and the US now being classified under neglect or emotional abuse. This appears to reflect a number of complex and interrelated factors. A host of troubles and sorrows suffered by children, young people and their families have been rendered subject to a child protection discourse that funnels understandings and responses in often very narrow and unhelpful ways. We have argued elsewhere that this may reflect the insatiability of a 'risk monster' that sees trouble and sorrow not as elements of the human condition exacerbated in particular contexts of disadvantage and inequality, but rather as evidence of risky choices or lifestyles (Featherstone et al, 2016). The research evidence on how such misrecognition impacts on families and professionals highlights the obstacles it places in the way of constructing meaningful narratives and engaging in transformative understandings (see Chapter four). This is very damaging. As Cottam (2011) observes, the ability to tell a story of where you have come from and where you hope to go, is a significant indicator of progress and of resilience.

Bunting et al (2017) argue that the growth in registered child protection cases of neglect and emotional abuse may reflect system imperatives in a context of competition for funding and resourcing. They argue that, if designating cases as abuse brings greater access to limited resources, social workers may define families' troubles in ways that increase the numbers of abuse and neglect cases. Thus, while the conditions of children's lives may not actually have changed, service responses have. Webb and Bywaters (2018) note that, since 2010, it is family support and early help services that have been cut substantially in order to manage the increased demand and reduced funding. Effectively there has been an unspoken, undiscussed policy change, rebalancing services away from family support at a time when families and services have faced exceptional pressures. In 2010 almost half of all children's services spend went on supporting families, with the other half on safeguarding and LAC services. Now, child protection and LAC involve over 70% of total spend.

On being designated a 'child protection case', families are engaged with by practice methodologies and processes that appear little attuned to place or context. It is, indeed, a paradox that, although children's and families' troubles are approached on a case-by-case basis, they are so often offered a routinised and formulaic menu. Methodologies are focused on effecting family or parental change and repeated monitoring visits by social workers form the lynchpin of protection processes. The results of such visits are then shared in multi-agency forums where families are too often reduced to the status of bystanders in their own lives.

To summarise, a story that was rooted in compassion towards the vulnerable in a Keynesian era has morphed into a highly blaming and risk-focused enterprise. Since 2010, and the active policies directed at reducing state support, the focus on the individual family and/or parent has become ethically problematic. In a context of the continued stripping away of many of the key supports necessary to ensure children and their families flourish (such as decent incomes, family-friendly working, quality public transport services, adequate housing and local support services) an individualised risk-focused practice culture reinforces rather than ameliorates the struggles families face.

Indeed, a disconnect is increasingly apparent, allowing governments to claim they are improving child protection while simultaneously promoting and implementing policies that increase the numbers of children living in poverty, reduce the support services available to them, and reinforce the inequalities that limit their potential. This disconnect was most painfully exposed in the summer of 2017 when fire tore through Grenfell Tower, a high rise block of flats in the richest borough in one of the richest cities in the world. Many watched aghast as it became clear the most basic duty of care owed to citizens had been breached in the construction of these homes, and as the response failed miserably to engage with the needs of terrified and traumatised survivors. This was compounded for those who knew this council had received the highest possible grade for its child protection services to children and families by the Office for Standards in Education,

Children's Services and Skills (OFSTED) (Stevenson, 2016). Yet all the while, the dangers in Grenfell Tower were hiding in plain sight. By exclusively focusing on intra-familial harm, extraordinarily destructive social and material harms became irrelevant to the child protection system.

A new story with some familiar chapters

In the wake of the financial crash, and the subsequent recession, the task of thinking beyond Keynesianism and the rise of neoliberalism has acquired an added impetus for a range of thinkers. There is now an urgency as they explore the consequences of the growth in inequalities and its implications for societal well-being, physical and mental health, a precarious economy and ecology, and a centralised state too often wedded to command-and-control modes of governance (see, for example, Cottam, 2011, Gillies et al, 2017).

Across a range of disciplines common cause is being made in arguing for a new social settlement that charts alternative policy directions to those of recent decades. We locate our work examining child protection within this rethinking and here sketch out its key aspects within what we have chosen to call a social model. Namely, that we must become preoccupied by:

- understanding and tackling root causes;
- rethinking the role of the state;
- developing relationship(s)-based practice and co-production; and
- embedding a dialogic approach to ethics and human rights in policy and practice.

This is difficult terrain to traverse. We want to unsettle the current story, reminiscent of 'underclass' discourses, in which blame for inequality is carried by flawed agentic individuals (Lister and Bennett, 2010) and where parenting, disconnected from social circumstance, is the site for intervention. However, there are a number of dangers attendant on our project that we wrestle with in the book and on which we invite further dialogue as part of expanding the audiences we seek to engage. There is a danger, for example, that we simply invert the status quo and substitute an 'underdog' story which presents those experiencing inequality as structurally constrained and lacking any potency and agency or responsibility for their troubles. For us, this polarised analysis is conceptually inadequate in advancing understandings of, and responses to, inequalities and associated 'harms'. There is, instead, a complex interplay between structure and agency. We invoke structure and agency here to resuscitate a sociologically informed social work and to create the possibility that social work may inform social scientific thought. We join with C. Wright Mills to argue that the most helpful distinction with which the sociological imagination must grapple is that between private troubles and public issues:

> Do not allow public issues as they are officially formulated, or troubles as they are privately felt, to determine the problems that you take up for study. Above all, do not give up your moral and political autonomy by accepting in somebody else's terms the illiberal practicality of the bureaucratic ethos or the liberal practicality of the moral scatter. Know that many personal troubles cannot be solved merely as troubles, but must be understood in terms of public issues – and in terms of the problems of history making. Know that the human meaning of public issues must be revealed by relating them to personal troubles – and to the problems of the individual life. Know that the problems of social science, when adequately formulated, must include both troubles and issues, both biography and history, and the range of their intricate relations. (Mills, 1959 [2000]: 226)

A further danger is that we contribute to a good family/bad professional binary. We argued in *Re-imagining Child Protection* for the importance of exploring and understanding 'double suffering', a phrase that encapsulates the reality that those who are harmed and discriminated against are not ennobled in the process. Workers are too often engaging with those who are hurt and hurting, angry and suspicious, defensive and defended. What we are seeking to do in this book is to rescue our thinking and practices from a seeming inability to see beyond superficial tropes such as 'they are making risky choices or they have poor attachment patterns'. We also want a move away from high challenge/low support approaches and to continue to interrogate what personal responsibility means to individuals, those who hurt and are hurting, and how it can be exercised meaningfully in varying contexts.

We consider a social model is of value as a rallying call and have been inspired by how thinking across a range of fields, including disability and mental health, has been challenged by the various social models that have emerged. It specifically draws attention to the economic, environmental and cultural barriers faced by people with differing levels of (dis)ability. This is a central project for those concerned with protecting children – what are the economic, environmental and cultural barriers to ensuring children are cared for safely, and their relational needs and identities respected? Attending to these barriers would mark a significant shift in orientation away from the current project of repeated home visiting to investigate and assess individual risk, backed up, where available, by services designed to effect change in family or parental functioning. It would start very different conversations about multi-agency working and community-based approaches, conversations that did begin to happen under the Every Child Matters Agenda of New Labour but were stymied by top-down target-driven modes of governance (Frost and Parton, 2009).

In the following chapters we seek to explore in detail the theoretical and empirical work that can build fresh thinking. Here, we signal the key elements in our approach and their importance:

Understanding and tackling root causes

In this book we seek to highlight particular aspects of the growing scholarship on inequality and poverty that we consider very neglected currently and highly pertinent to rethinking child protection policy and practice. We are very aware that it is but a start and that there is far more work to be done to understand how poverty and inequality are experienced by individual men, women, boys and girls, gay, straight and transgender and of differing ethnicities and (dis)abilities, and thus intersect with gender, 'race', disability and sexuality.

Bauman captures beautifully the relational dimensions of poverty when he notes: 'The poor will always be with us, but what it means to be poor depends on the kind of "us" they are "with"' (Bauman, quoted in Friedli, 2009: 38). The importance of the social and psychological dimensions of material deprivation is gaining greater recognition in the international literature and informs current efforts to develop indicators that capture the missing dimensions of poverty (Friedli, 2009: iii). An extensive body of research confirms the relationship between inequality and poorer outcomes, a relationship that is evident at every position on the social hierarchy. The emotional and cognitive effects of high levels of social status differentiation are profound and far reaching: greater inequality heightens status competition and status insecurity across all income groups and among both adults and children. It is the distribution of economic and social resources that explains health and other outcomes in the vast majority of studies.

This kind of thinking is not at all common in child protection despite its relevance. As Wilkinson and Pickett (2009: 111), leading researchers on inequality and its impacts, note:

> In Chapter 4 we described how the general quality of social relationships is lower in more unequal societies, and in Chapters 5 and 6 we showed how inequality is linked to poorer physical and mental health and more substance misuse. It's not a great leap then to think how life in a more hierarchical, mistrustful society might affect intimate, domestic, relationships and family life. Domestic conflict and violence, parental mental illness, poverty of time and resources will all combine to affect child development.

However, our research in the child protection system has found evidence of the disembedding of the miseries of depression, drinking too much and violence, for example, from their social determinants. Instead they are constructed as individualised risky behaviours locked in a toxic embrace (Morris et al, 2017). This is apparent in the widespread and very sloppy use of the term 'the toxic trio'. The term comes from a particular, very specific, context but has morphed alarmingly. It emerged from successive analyses of serious case reviews of child deaths that highlighted the interrelationship between domestic violence, mental ill-health and substance misuse (Brandon et al, 2012). In an analysis of 184 serious case reviews carried out over a two-year period, it was found that all three factors were present in just over a fifth of cases and that it was the combination of these factors which was particularly 'toxic'.

It is of concern, however, that we have found the term is used when it is not clear that all three types of problem are, in fact, present in a family. In accounts from social workers and managers, it seems to operate as a heuristic, a mental shortcut that not only eases the cognitive load of making a decision, but unhelpfully conflates very diverse phenomena and fails to engage with the subjective meanings attached to such behaviours as well as the evidence on their social determinants (see Morris et al, 2017 and Chapter seven of this book).

Writers from within a social harms, as well as an inequalities, perspective offer very pertinent insights for those seeking to move away from an emphasis on individualised risk factors towards understanding and locating these in a wider canvass:

> The approach that we have sought may encompass the detrimental activities of local and national states and of corporations on the welfare of individuals, whether this be lack of wholesome food, inadequate housing or heating, low income, exposure to various forms of danger, violations of basic human rights, and victimisation to various forms of crime. Of course, when we speak of people's welfare, we refer not (simply) to an atomised individual, or to men and women and their families, the social units who often experience harm. For it is clear that various forms of harms are not distributed randomly, but fall upon people of different social classes, genders, degrees of physical ability, racial and ethnic groups, different ages, sexual preferences, and so on. (Dorling et al, 2008: 14)

As Gillies et al (2017: 169) note, rather than attempting to calculate individual risk, social harm theorists identify collective responses to personal injuries. This approach enables a much wider investigation of precipitating factors and accountability, as well as an appreciation of the consequences of governments failing to act to address deprivation or corporate exploitation. A social harms lens reveals that the most pervasive and intractable social injuries derive from the pursuit of particular political and policy directions rather than intentional actions or personal deficits. We return to this perspective further in Chapter five.

Rethinking the state

'During the Keynesian area, the state was the institution to which people turned for protection from exploitation and arbitrary power. Today, it is perceived as an agent of exploitation and arbitrary power' (Monbiot, 2017: 59). Monbiot's analysis ignores the ways in which the welfare state reinforced inequalities in relation to gender and 'race' but he captures an important set of concerns about the state today. As Judt (2011) notes, the reduction of public services has actually increased the unrestrained powers of the over-mighty state, reducing connections with it and investment by citizens, and increasing alienation and/or fear and suspicion.

Loic Wacquant (2010) has argued that the role of the 'night-watchman' state in managing the working class and the poor has been expanded and aggressively strengthened under neoliberalism. He outlines the development of a 'centaur state' (see also Parton, 2014).

The centaur state presents a 'comely and caring visage towards the middle and upper classes, and a fearsome and frowning mug towards the lower class' (Wacquant, 2010: 217). In this new model, the state has retreated from a number of areas, most notably the regulation of the market, but for the urban poor the scope and extent of state regulation has increased.

This analysis by Wacquant can help to locate some of the empirical findings around how child protection systems operate that have emerged in recent times. There has been a steady increase in the numbers of families experiencing investigations for suspected abuse in the last decades, the majority of which do not appear to uncover actual abuse and/or result in help being offered to families. This is a trend across a range of anglophone countries but if we focus on England we see that investigations increased by 79.4%, in the period from 2009/2010 to 2014/2015 (Bilson and Martin, 2016). Did this reflect increases in actual abuse? While the numbers on child protection plans did rise, this rise of 40.5% fell far below those actually investigated. Moreover, because there are no statistics on the numbers who move from investigation to help or support services, it is difficult to assess how any needs that were uncovered in the course of an investigation were dealt with. This rise has been attributed to the crisis after the death of Peter Connolly. However, a number of research studies now suggest this crisis appeared to fuel a pre-existing trend in the increased use of child protection investigations to deal with demands on services (see Hood et al, 2016).

Thus, need has become refracted through a risk prism. This impacts disproportionately on the poorest children and their families according to Bilson et al (2017). They estimated the proportion of children in a class of 30 born between 1 April 2009 and 31 March 2010 who had reached various stages of children's services involvement before their fifth birthday from areas in the tenth decile of deprivation. They noted that for a significant number of deprived children, it is conceivable their first encounter with the state (apart from universal health services) is via a Section 47 investigation.[1] This needs to be considered alongside the evidence presented above on the links between deprivation and LAC rates and suggests a landscape where deprived communities are bearing the scars of investigations and removals with untold consequences for all concerned.

It is also important to note the gendered implications, with women, often lone parents, the focus of much activity reflecting inequalities

---

[1]   Section 47 of the Children Act 1989 refers to investigation of suspected abuse.

in terms of poverty and sexual violence. As we will explore further in the book, this activity, in the main, fails to deal with their poverty and vulnerabilities and, indeed, may reinforce them.

It is important to stress that we are absolutely committed to an invigorated vision for the state at both local and national levels and offer a range of possibilities at conceptual, policy and practice levels for realising this vision. Many key features of children's and families' welfare can only be secured through robust action by the state at local and national levels; tackling inequality and providing and regulating incomes, housing, health and education. There is also a vital monitoring and auditing role for the state in relation to issues such as inequality of opportunities and outcomes, and in this context it is of concern that no government across the UK collects data on the economic and social circumstances of the families who become involved in child protection systems (Bywaters et al, 2018).

But, as we explore throughout this book, in the area of child protection it is urgent that we move beyond reliance on state services and top-down approaches to protect children and ensure their welfare and safety and that we embed robust community and locality-based engagement in all our endeavours.

Relationship(s)-based practice and co-production

Considerable critical attention in the last decade focused on the mode of governance developed under New Labour. This attention was indeed necessary, even if the overall project was limited as it neglected, for example, systematic patterns of state practices. A very centralised model of governance instituted a regime of targets and metrics leading to considerable concern, not least in relation to the hollowing out of relationships between practitioners and families in transactional encounters.

Against this backdrop, relationship-based practice has become the sine qua non of professional discourses, invested in by very different constituencies. We welcome this interest, but it is often too narrowly focused on the relationships between professional workers and families and interpersonal dynamics. Paradoxically, it overestimates the importance of the worker while underestimating her power, and pays too little attention to the wider relationships necessary for families to flourish and thus to promoting practices that increase connections with neighbours, networks and communities.

Our analysis suggests the importance of rethinking and understanding relationships and developing practices that promote a broad and imaginative project. This is not only a pragmatic necessity given levels of distrust between the state, professionals and families, but is rooted in a growing evidence base on the importance of social relations to health and well-being and the damage caused by social isolation and loneliness:

> The significance of mental health and its role in our survival confirms the importance of humans as social beings: levels of social interaction are universal determinants of wellbeing across all cultures. But the unique nature of each person's mental character also reminds us of the power of the individual: *'no one survives without community and no community thrives without the individual'*. (Friedli, 2009: iv, emphasis in original)

Monbiot (2017: 24) argues for the need for reconnection and restoration as part of a new settlement through reviving community: 'By reviving community, built around the places in which we live, and by anchoring ourselves, our politics and parts of our economy in the life of this community, we can recover the best aspects of our humanity.'

While it is customary and, indeed, appropriate to interrogate and rethink notions of community, especially when conflated with place, we would argue that there are really important issues being highlighted by Monbiot. There does seem to be considerable evidence to suggest that community ties impact, positively and negatively, on a host of issues, from the safety of particular streets, to the life expectancy of the people who live on them (Clark with Heath, 2014).

However, Clark with Heath (2014: 131) highlight the challenges in the contemporary context, coining the term 'the social recession' to describe the fall away in volunteering and engagement in community life in the context of the economic recession since 2008. Their conclusions are important:

> The Great Recession stifled spontaneous kindness right across England, but did so more aggressively in the communities that started out poor. Some element of speculation is inescapably involved in explaining why. Increasingly insecure work in poor towns, which cannot be easily identified and controlled for in the same way as unemployment, could be a big part of this tale: it may cause people to become withdrawn, or it could make it harder to commit their time. But however the link works, it would

appear that the reckoning for those long decades in which the Barnsleys, the Liverpools and the Nottinghams were left behind economically finally arrived in the wake of the Great Recession. Social ties that had very gradually frayed in such places proved especially susceptible to hard times. And these, of course, are the very boroughs where people have often got nothing apart from each other.

They contrast the picture in the US and the UK with a very different one in France and Germany and reflect that it looks as though 'community' is yet another dimension of life in the Anglo-Saxon economies through which the recession tore a selective path, bearing down on those already wounded. Moreover, they caution those wounds may harden into lasting social scars.

In such circumstances can communities be mobilised as part of protecting children, or are they simply too fragile, damaged and mistrusted? We think there is actually no alternative to trying different ways of thinking and doing *with* rather than *to* families and their communities. We can no longer go on as remote professionals visiting from afar in our cars but we recognise it is a long slow grind in the context of histories of fear and lack of trust. One vital element of the approach we advocate is co-production.

We recognise child protection has a fragile history of sustained movements for change that are led by those requiring child protection interventions and that othering, shame and stigma present real barriers to building alliances between politicians, professionals and families (Warner, 2015). But it is our hope that this book can be a contribution towards growing and strengthening the possibilities of co-production. We offer examples through the book, based on our own work, and that of others, of projects that are either involved in co-production or could be with support.

We also note the learning from other countries where marginalised communities have been particularly impacted by child investigations and removals. Feminists, such as Joan Pennell (Pennell and Kim, 2010) in the US, work within restorative justice, noting that state responses to violence and child abuse have led to mother blaming and child removal and there has been a reliance on legal interventions that often backfire on poor women and women of colour. She has been concerned with whether advocates for women and children can collaborate with state institutions without becoming co-opted to goals that run counter to their beliefs. We explore her work in Chapter seven in relation to domestic abuse and highlight the importance of the initiatives she has developed in promoting and fostering strengths and resources within families and communities. We consider these hold possibilities for both using aspects of the state's power and building up countervailing and resilient resources that are rooted in connection and relationality and very firmly eschew practices that increase social isolation and loneliness.

Restorative approaches are enjoying a very welcome surge of attention and interest in the UK currently. We would suggest that their undoubted contribution could be strengthened by being more securely anchored in socio-economic analyses of the factors impacting on social capital in particular areas. It is here that the state, including at a local level, can play a vital role. For example, across the UK, Fairness or Equality Commissions have been set up to work with communities on tackling and reducing inequality at local levels (New Economics Foundation, 2015). These have mobilised politicians alongside a wide variety of actors to conduct audits on pay, housing, education and so on. To date we are not aware of any that explicitly consider what is needed to protect children. We consider these audits could be revised to include work on indicators that contribute directly to inequalities for children in terms of being to live safely and flourish within their families of origin and communities and to nurture conversations in relation to the following:

- Do families across communities have sufficient income to meet basic care needs and if not how is this impacting on levels of demand for services?
- What are the work opportunities available and is there affordable childcare?
- Is there adequate and affordable housing?
- What do families say they need to care adequately for their children?
- How safe do they consider their environments, the streets they live in, the parks and public spaces available to them?
- What services do they want?
- Where are the mechanisms for their involvement in service design and commissioning?
- How are families involved in discussing their experiences of these services?
- What is life like on their street? Their estate?
- Do they often feel lonely? Who can they talk to? Where do they feel safe and nurtured?
- What opportunities are there to develop respectful and nurturing relationships between the genders and across ages and ethnicities?

Embedding ethics and human rights: a dialogic approach

In a recent enquiry on the role of the social worker in adoption, it emerged that a language of ethics and human rights was underdeveloped in social work, the lead profession in child protection (Featherstone et al, 2018). This is not surprising as it does seem as if the language of evidence and outcomes has colonised the available discursive space. We think it is vital to recognise that attention to evidence is itself central to ethical practice but too often we see it used in a way that reinforces the instrumentalism we identified in *Re-imagining Child Protection* (Featherstone et al, 2014). By instrumentalism we meant the following: people (particularly mothers) were treated as means rather than ends and discussions were too often solely about 'what works' rather than broader reflections about ends, means, where personal responsibility begins and ends, the nature of a good society, and so on. We think there is a need to strengthen such discussions and to draw from the now-extensive literature on ethics and human rights.

The notion of 'ethical trespass' refers to the reality that many practice situations are those where no correct response is clear or indeed entirely right (Weinberg and Campbell, 2014). Moreover, they involve multiple stakeholders, such that what is right for one member of a family may not be for another, and complex considerations about principles, consequences, means and ends need to be engaged with. This underlines the need for ethical talk to be embedded in organisational cultures of reflection and dialogue. However, in the enquiry on adoption we found little evidence that such cultures were routinely available to those practising in child protection and, indeed, found the enquiry itself became a resource for ethical talk for those deprived of other possibilities (see Featherstone et al, 2018).

We found that there was little reference to codes of ethics such as those developed by professional organisations. Is it that, as has been argued by Weinberg and Campbell (2014), these are too abstract and do not address the need to engage with issues and relationships in particular contexts? This merits further exploration.

Weinberg (2009) draws attention to the notion of 'moral distress' and its importance. This theoretical concept identifies the psychological and emotional pain that arises when professionals feel blocked from doing what they consider is morally correct, due to constraints outside the self. She argues that it needs to be distinguished from the concept of ethical dilemma.

Ethical dilemmas concern two or more courses of action that are in conflict (and will potentially have both positive and negative consequences), each of which can be defended as viable and appropriate. In contrast, moral distress arises if one action is preferred and seen as superior, but the person feels blocked from pursuing it by a range of factors. Moral distress involves exploring the degree to which a worker views herself/himself as individually responsible or as restricted by circumstances.

Several important questions arise from this. How can we ensure practitioners retain a sense of personal agency? How can we build cultures that support them, recognising their personal responsibility for ethical practice and for challenging the barriers to ethical practice?

Those who experienced child protection practices told the enquiry of the use and misuse of power by child protection professionals and the impact of particular practices on already marginalised groups. A human rights perspective seems imperative in order to underscore the importance of access to good quality legal advice and independent advocacy and to the second generation of human rights: social and economic rights. However, we found little evidence that social workers used a human rights perspective although they identified many issues as of concern that involve human rights breaches. Would a language of human rights, or even natural justice, be more likely to promote human rights-informed practice? We think that language matters, constructing as well as reflecting, what can be thought about and how.

Ife (2012) argues that a human rights perspective provides a robust framing of 'practising ethically' for contemporary social work and identifies deductive and inductive approaches to human rights. Deductive approaches ask how constructions of human rights (for example, the European Convention on Human Rights) can be applied to specific situations. Inductive approaches require that human rights issues inherent in practice situations can be identified and analysed. Both approaches are important, but an inductive approach which frames private troubles as public issues (what are the human rights issues at stake for this child and family?) requires the acceptance of a political dimension to problems. We consider this discursive approach to human rights is consistent with a situated and contextualised view of ethics.

In the context of the concerns of this book, the interconnectedness of children's rights and human rights would appear to need much more robust discussion in social work in children's services. In the enquiry on adoption we found a tendency to assume that human rights were only applicable to adults and children's rights were separate if/ not counterpoised. We consider this is profoundly problematic and a misunderstanding of the UN Convention on the Rights of the Child (UNCRC).

Melton (2010: 162) notes that even though human rights law generally regulates the conduct of governments, not individual people, it is the province of all. He quotes US human rights advocate Eleanor Roosevelt who, when addressing the UN General Assembly, described where human rights begin: 'In small places, close to home – so close and so small they cannot be seen on any maps of the world. Yet they are the world of the individual person; the neighbourhood he lives in, the school or college he attends; the factory, farm, or office where he works.' Ms Roosevelt eloquently explained: 'Such are the places where every man, woman, and child seeks equal justice, equal opportunity, equal dignity without discrimination. Unless these rights have meaning there, they have little meaning anywhere' (Melton, 2010: 162). Ultimately, the core idea in international human rights law is universality. If human dignity is to be protected, then the humanity of every person must be recognised and respected. A key point made by Melton that is central to our thinking is his emphasis on the importance of relationships to rights and their interconnection. None of us are simply free-floating individuals but are part of, and enmeshed in, relationships – rights are exercised relationally and choices are considered contextually. We are therefore very concerned about tendencies to consider children's rights in narrowly individualised ways as this fosters a 'child rescue' approach which can fail to engage with the complexity of needs and identities over the life course.

In the next sections we offer some reflections on what our approach might look like in practice.

Stories of hope, repair and relationships: new directions

The following case studies illustrate some of the harmful experiences children, young people and their families may experience, highlight the customary responses in the current framework and offer some illustrations of what a social model might offer. These are composite case studies drawing from empirical data from a series of child welfare studies, allowing us to be confident that our discussions are rooted in children's lived experiences.

Early childhood

Aisha is 20yrs old and has given birth to her second child, Maya. Her first child (Taylor) lives with foster carers (with a plan for adoption) and the local authority has the necessary orders to remove Maya. Aisha lives in temporary accommodation and is completely reliant on welfare benefits. She and her maternal family are migrants, having fled war and famine in Libya, All have been granted residency in their country of choice; only her sister lives in the UK. The paternal family live in the UK and are all white UK citizens. Aisha was the subject of chronic domestic abuse from the outset of the relationship with Maya's father, who beat her during pregnancy. She smoked and drank throughout pregnancy and has remained ambivalent about her feelings towards Maya. She mourns deeply the loss of her first child (he had a different father, but one who also beat Aisha).

This case study describes concerns that the current system is best equipped to deal with. And, indeed, cases such as this one are dealt with very decisively with recent years seeing an increase in the use of compulsory measures at birth. This has occurred in the context of a very explicit push by successive governments to promote adoption (Featherstone et al, 2018).

Although removal and adoption may be assumed to work for Maya in the short term, they offer vivid illustrations of the pursuit of 'unsafe certainty', which has been such a feature of policies and practices and the focus of much concern. The focus on immediate safety needs is vital but, in our current system, it carries with it long-term risks of harm. In order to address these, any response must be located within a wider analysis that explores whether other options might both offer safety and safeguard her future well-being, including her needs for stability and her identity needs.

There is a role for the state, a role envisaged by the Children Act 1989, that is not always purposefully explored and implemented. It must be asked why we do not routinely provide respite fostering for mothers and children in these situations, not on a time-limited basis, but as part of an ongoing circle of support. We must protect vulnerable babies but, in order to do so and safeguard their rights over the life course, we must beware of a narrow rescue and rupture paradigm and consider the possibilities for repair and restoration.

Understanding the importance of repair and restoration is crucial, particularly for mothers such as Aisha, when we consider the relationship between individual biographies such as hers and the social processes attached to huge social changes such as forced migration. Frost and Hoggett (2008) note that experiences that have been forced on us rather than those we freely choose, those we face as powerless objects rather than as active agents, threaten to go beyond our capacity for thought and emotional processing. They argue that it is very damaging if we are not able to think about our experiences and make sense of them emotionally and intellectually. Indeed, in such circumstances, there are a number of very different possibilities for how we act/react. These include self-destructive behaviour (such as alcohol and substance misuse), behaviour that is damaging or harmful to places, and destructive and damaging behaviour towards others, including those more vulnerable.

Overall, while the removal of Maya via closed adoption may meet the needs of a particular calculative logic, it must be questioned from a perspective that considers ethical and human rights considerations for all concerned, including Maya herself.

Transition years

Michael is ten years old and lives in the poorest neighbourhood in his local authority. He attends junior school but will move to secondary school next year. He is white, UK born. His parents work shifts and thus he leaves the house on his own in the morning and often comes home to an empty house. He usually misses breakfast but his mum or dad try to sort out tea for him. He has health problems: he's asthmatic and has chronic gum disease and is obese. He has an older sister who looks after him when she isn't working shifts in a local shop. He doesn't do any homework, and he falls asleep sometimes in class because he likes to stay up late playing x-box. He doesn't go out to play because he's been bullied a lot at school and doesn't trust his 'friends' not to hurt him. Michael's mum and dad don't go into school because they feel intimidated and so they don't know he's had problems. Michael is withdrawn and unhappy, his teachers worry about him.

Michael would not meet the threshold currently for services in many parts of the country. As we noted previously there has been an unspoken policy shift from family support and early help to child protection investigations and removals, with spending on the former drastically reduced. But if a teacher were to manage to recast Michael's needs as risk successfully and thus prompt action, the most that would be likely to happen is that he and his parents would receive a one-off visit. This would usually be framed within an interrogation of his parents' actions or inactions, with little recognition of the impact of precarious working on parents' capacities, or of the wider social determinants of Michael's poor health and well-being. Indeed Morris et al (2018a) note child protection social workers often explicitly rule out such considerations in their assessments. But placing Michael's troubles within a child protection frame puts more pressure on parents who are already struggling and is likely to add to their feelings of shame.

An alternative approach as part of a social model would explore with Michael himself what he considers he needs and how his rights can be respected and nurtured in line with the UNCRC. As explored further in this book, it would also mean developing local services that are rooted in an understanding of the work patterns of local parents, the pressures on them and, rather than wasting resources on frightening and unhelpful Section 47 enquiries, would support the development of good-quality neighbourhood-based facilities for children and young people and their families. These could be developed by and with a variety of community-based and faith organisations. Such facilities could support a range of objectives – tackling bullying and supporting gender-informed approaches that recognise the often differing vulnerabilities of boys and girls. This is about shared collective experiences within communities, and building services in response to these is a far cry from the current distant (geographically as well as emotionally) investigative services that form the core of our current responses to children's harms.

Young people and harm

Sasha is 16 years old, mixed heritage (her father was from Ireland and her mother from Poland) and lives in a small residential unit in a large city. She entered the care system when she was 11, and this is her sixth placement. She is described as volatile and difficult. She was sexually abused at home by her stepfather and has had no contact with any family members since removal into care when she was 11. She has lost touch with her two siblings (both boys) who are older than her and did not enter the care system. She has friends who also live at the unit and they spend time with a local group of older men. There are serious concerns that she may be involved with child sexual exploitation (CSE).

In recent years CSE has exposed some of the fault lines in our current approaches to understanding and dealing with the harms children and young people experience and this is to be welcomed. The work of Pearce (2013) is of great importance here. She also sees the need for a social model and uses it to consider issues of consent in relation to CSE. She presents four areas where professionals and others supporting the child and young person should focus their attention on understanding the structural and cultural contexts of the abuse. They could look at whether the child or young person is:

1. being groomed into sexual exploitation and abuse by adults or other children;
2. experiencing poverty and therefore engaging in what has been termed 'survival sex';
3. influenced by the 'normalisation of sexual violence' as projected through violent pornography and/or through peer group patterns that accept violence as part of everyday life;
4. overlooked or ignored by a culture of 'wilful ignorance', where professionals or others in contact with the child turn away from the truth of what is happening.

The current child protection system has struggled with CSE partly because of the assumption that the harms children and young people need protecting from are normally located within individual families and are caused by actions of omission or commission by adult caretakers. Thus, in terms of practice by child protection services, in some of the cases that have emerged in recent years it often appeared there was no legitimate frame within which to place the child or young person. They could not be constructed as a 'child protection case' because the child protection system intervened only with families where harm was occurring. Indeed in some debates and practice responses it appeared the young people became subject to the trope of 'exercising life style choices' so in that case there was no need for social workers in child protection to be concerned with them. Often these highly vulnerable young people only became of interest to the child protection systems if they got pregnant and it was their babies that were then 'the victims', with the mother of concern only in so far as she met the child's needs.

Moreover, where parents were considered it was as part of the problem, although parents were often desperate for help, desperate to be partners in protection and were themselves victimised by forces way beyond their control. Any acknowledgment of wider issues came through the notion of community engagement, which became outsourced to local leaders rather than being seen as a core element in protecting children and young people.

But there is another approach possible and evident in some areas, an approach that often is not considered 'proper child protection' – an approach that engages young people at their own pace, holds risk sensitively, works in communities, strengthens community capacities to understand and address the harms children and young people experience. In this book, we propose building on these traditions and supporting parents and family networks to understand what is going on, to draw strength from each other and prevent younger children from being caught up in cycles of harm. We suggest that such practices should be core business in a social model of protecting children and young people.

Concluding remarks: travelling hopefully?

> It is important to say what hope is not: it is not the belief that everything was, is, or will be fine. The evidence is all around us of tremendous suffering and destruction. The hope I am interested in is about broad perspectives with specific possibilities, ones that invite or demand that we act. It is also not a sunny everything-is-getting-better narrative, though it may be a counter to the everything-is-getting-worse one. You could call it an account of complexities and uncertainties, with openings. 'Critical thinking without hope is cynicism, but hope without critical thinking is naivety,' the Bulgarian writer Maria Popova recently remarked. (Solnit, 2016: xi/ii)

Our project is rooted in hope and critical thinking. Thus, let us restate some of the possible dangers with what we are saying. Are we promoting one model? Does the focus on the social reduce individuals to ciphers, reductive instances of the general? Are we, therefore, reinforcing a damaging binary? What about personal responsibility and individual agency?

We see the social model as signalling an orientation rather than a simple model and recognise the term may therefore be misleading. Its use on our part is strategic to some extent, signalling a profound challenge to what has become an increasingly inward-looking focus on brains, psyches and individual homes. But it is also a very positive choice too as it signposts the importance of recognising and promoting what is central to our humanity: our interdependence, our basic needs for financial resources, a warm place to live, enough to eat, love and respect.

We consider it important to eschew the dichotomising of social structure and individual agency (Weinberg, 2009). Society is the creation of human beings, and social structures are made and remade through practices. Every time an individual enacts practice in a particular way, what constitutes child protection, for example, is constructed at that moment.

Moreover, our subjectivity is formed in and through relationships, and our ties and commitments to others mean practices such as 'exercising responsibility' are practices undertaken by moral selves in particular contexts.

Over 30 years ago Dingwall et al (1983: 244) coined these wise words:

> [C]hild protection raises complex moral and political issues which have no one right technical solution. Practitioners are asked to solve problems everyday that philosophers have argued about the last two thousand years ... Moral evaluations can and must be made if children's lives and wellbeing are to be secured. What matters is that we should not disguise this and pretend it is all a matter of finding better checklists or new models of psychopathology – technical fixes when the proper decision is a decision about what constitutes a good society.

Our project is animated by a desire to place questions about what constitutes a good society at the heart of our concerns and, in the chapters that follow, we explore further why we think 'child protection' needs to be remade fundamentally in the interests of protecting children and building a good society for them and those who care for, and about, them.

Structure of the book

Chapters Two and Three explore not only the background to our current travails but offer vital pointers towards the direction of travel if there is not change. The gaze will, we argue, become more and more inwardly focused, seeking biomarkers for disadvantage and danger and taking us further and further away from collective approaches rooted in care and solidarity. Chapter four builds on recent research projects by the authors to explore the often highly damaging and unhelpful service responses experienced by families. In Chapters five and six we explore what a social model means conceptually and in terms of policy and practice with a particular focus in Chapter seven on domestic abuse. Chapter eight, using framing theory, offers a range of tools for deconstructing and interrogating current stories and highlights how we might counter these and develop new stories as part of the movement for change. In the conclusion we signpost the conversations that need to happen to make change begin to seem like a possibility.

TWO

Trouble ahead? Contending discourses in child protection

> If the last 150 years of social thought has taught anything, it is that our understanding of normality is more a product of historical provincialism than genuinely universal intuitions. Thus, a critical sense of sympathy serves as a reminder that the proper object of sympathy is a common *future* co-habitable by ourselves and others to whom we would extend sympathy regardless of the differences that most immediately strike us .... (Fuller, 2006: 120 emphasis in original)

In this chapter, using the UK[2] system as an exemplar, we consider the history of attempts to improve the way families look after children. We trace the current child protection system and its twists and turns. As we have argued in the Introduction, more and more of the sorrows of life are being defined as the proper business of a child welfare system predicated on surveillance. While the state and its resources allegedly shrink, its gaze is harder and its tongue sharper. As part of an increasingly residual role, the system has become narrowly focused on an atomised child, severed from family, relationships and social circumstances: a precarious object of 'prevention', or rescue. As its categories and definitions have gradually grown, the gap between child protection services and family support, or ordinary help, has, somewhat paradoxically, widened. This has a number of antecedents. First, with the exception of a few decades of the 20th century, history shows a strong tendency towards individual social engineering to produce model citizens, with parenting practices the primary focus of state attention. Second, a version of evidence and expertise has flourished in which interventions become analogous to doses of a drug, with clearly delineated packages delivered over strict time scales. Third, the post-war welfare consensus has withered in the face of market enchantment and a burgeoning commissioning paradigm. Fourth and

---

[2] While we recognise that devolution has resulted in some divergence in policies and practices, the overall trajectory in relation to child protection is remarkably similar we would suggest.

finally, the logics of managerial efficiency have flourished and, in a climate of reduced public spending, are king. These things together create intellectual apartheid (Midgley, 2013), with perfectly valid and vital understandings of life squeezed out of the policy, and increasingly the practice, sphere. We begin by summarising key moments in the early history of child protection, tracing, from these to the present day, a great leap backwards.

Child protection and expertise: enduring stories

Young and Ashton (1956) document the history of child protection and adoption services in Britain during the 19th century. Several developments at that time disrupted the liberal principle of non-interference in the decisions that families made about the care (or indeed otherwise) of their children. In 1875, the New York Society for the Prevention of Cruelty to Children was established, in the wake of publicity about the severe maltreatment of Mary Ellen, a fostered child. There followed a determined campaign to introduce a similar society in England. This was achieved in Liverpool in 1883 and a year later in London. Other towns followed and a nascent national society was formed in 1889. In 1895 the national society obtained a Royal Charter and additional power and influence. The society sought to lobby for legislative change and to intervene directly in families where children were harmed or deemed to be in some danger. 1889 saw the enactment of the Prevention of Cruelty to, and Protection of, Children Act, 'the Children's Charter'. This made it an offence for any person with care of a child to ill-treat, abandon or neglect that child. It also gave the court powers to remove a child to a place of safety. The police were given powers to remove children without a court order, these were extended to officers of the National Society for the Prevention of Cruelty to Children (NSPCC) in 1904. In 1889, boards of guardians were given powers to assume parental rights if a child had been deserted or the parents incarcerated because they had committed an offence against the child. This established a mechanism for a person other than the birth parent to become the child's legal guardian while that parent was still alive and without their consent. The 1891 Custody of Children Act ('Barnardo Act') arose because of public outcry over the cases of 'Roddy' and 'Gossage', in which the parents had requested that Dr Barnardo take the children into care, but subsequently asked for them to be returned. Ensuing legal action found in the parents' favour. The Act reversed this presumption, giving the court the power to consider the parents' 'character' and to take into consideration that that they had wilfully abandoned, deserted or flagrantly neglected the child. Thus, a temporary decision to ask for a child to be looked after by a charitable organisation could become a permanent one through administrative fiat – a situation that is currently enjoying renewed policy appeal in England.

The 19th-century legal developments were clearly driven by passionate reformers. Writing at the time of the Mary Ellen case in New York, Rev A. Morton recounts the matter being brought before the court, noting that 'strong men who looked on that battered little body wept like children, and wondered how they had been blind to it all for so many years' (Young and Ashton, 1956: 149). Thus, there are always compelling moral reasons to act to prevent, or stop, cruelty to children.

But, the social circumstances of the families were also characterised by profound poverty and appalling living conditions. The work of the NSPCC officers in preventing cruelty and supervising those families where cruelty was deemed to have occurred was thus:

> partly admonitory, and partly concerned with welfare … If on inquiry cruelty were evident, the officers did not necessarily bring the matter before the Justices at once. but by warning and exhortation, sought to frighten, or persuade the parents to moderate their behaviour … The admonitory method used by the N.S.P.C.C. officials was by no means their only one. For, in order to prevent cruelty, or to build up a family after a court sentence, some positive case-work was necessary. There is no doubt that by kindness and common sense these officers did some excellent work in this respect. Nor was this work on the plane of material relief, as the N.S.P.C.C. never became a relief society. (Young and Ashton, 1956: 151)

There are some recurring themes, to which we will in due course attend. The 19th century saw a real separation of the protection of children from the alleviation of poverty and general social support. Yet, the actions of the early NSPCC inspectors suggest that there is no necessary contradiction between acting to protect children and providing a compassionate and understanding response to families. However, compassion is not a neutral emotion. With sensitivity to the suffering of children came increasing levels of surveillance of the homes and lives of less fortunate members of society, with the NSPCC officers popularly dubbed 'the cruelty' men (Ferguson, 2011).

A concern in civil society with child cruelty caught the moral tide in the late 19th and early 20th centuries, which saw the dawn of progressive movements of various kinds, aimed broadly at the promotion of public health, the control of communicative disease and improvements to sanitation (Bridges, 1928). The mental hygiene movement also formed a significant strand in these developments, originating in 1908 (Bridges, 1928) and marking an aspirational shift from concern with disease to concern with prevention of both personal and social malaise. The responsibility of parents to provide an optimal environment for their child was foundational:

> [mental hygiene] ... consists first in providing for the birth of children endowed with good brains, denying as far as possible, the privilege of parenthood to the manifestly unfit who are almost certain to transmit bad nervous systems to their offspring ... and second, in supplying all individuals, from the moment of fusion of the parental germ-cells onward, and whether ancestrally well begun or not, with the environment best suited for the welfare of their mentality. (Beers, 1921: 299)

By granting early infant experience leavening power over adult functioning, the state was able to claim new mandates. Ambitions for social improvement have the advantage of appeal to both conservative and reforming constituencies. For conservatives, intervention would prevent moral decline and encourage gainful economic activity to support the established order. For progressive and radical campaigners, it appeared to challenge the idea that the poor are simply the poor and nothing could, or should, be done to help them (Young and Ashton, 1956). For progressive thinkers, an argument for the role of the state in improving the lives of children was welcome. Prevention was born.

The need for intervention to ensure the child's optimum progression thus naturally fell into its allotted place. The visceral revulsion about extreme child cruelty such as that endured by Mary Ellen in New York coalesced with a project of moral and psychological regulation:

> Many children of poor urban families arrive in school minimally prepared for academic instruction ... many of these children have great difficulty learning to read. Everyone agrees on the necessity of benevolent intervention to persuade the mothers of these children to adopt the

regular practices of middle class parents, playing with and talking to their children. (Kagan, 1998: 89)

There are hard-wearing continuities to the present day. The early years of a child's life continue to have a pivotal significance in welfare policy and practice, giving rise to the dominance of developmental psychology in professional, and indeed lay, ideas about childhood, and so about the responsibilities of parenthood. The allure of 'infant determinism' rests on the conviction that 'every experience produces a permanent change somewhere in the central nervous system and therefore the earliest experiences provide the scaffolding for the child's future thought and behaviour' (Kagan, 1998: 86).

There are particularly potent examples at work, with a contemporary global concern with the effects of Adverse Childhood Experiences (ACEs), which we will discuss in more detail in due course. Infant determinism is a strong policy song. It is arguably currently enjoying a reinvigorated and enthusiastic cantillation, but other stories are silenced, and possibilities lost in its entrancing, utopian cadences.

A better Britain for child, family and community: a sojourn in the mid-20th century

The post-war welfare consensus in Britain provided a brief respite from the policy preoccupation with the idle and feckless on the one hand and the vulnerable on the other. The sacrifices of the population during World War 2 produced a policy promise of a better Britain for everyone. The wartime coalition government had produced a series of White Papers proposing a national health service, expanded universal education and social housing, ideas that were quickly brought to fruition.

In this context, social work became reputable and legitimised. The new focus for government was the reduction of complexity in service provision, and a range of disparate and overlapping services were brought into public governance. The 1968 Seebohm Report advocated a change of focus from individual deficits to community needs and rights (Donnison, 1969). Families were to be helped through generic social services based in local authorities. No longer the province of 'the cruelty men', child protection would become part of this therapeutically oriented venture (Ferguson, 2011). The cradle-to-grave approach adopted by generic services within the welfare consensus offered the possibility for delivering enduring practical help for those who had difficulties with everyday coping, albeit in the context of increasingly bureaucratic organisations (Parton, 2014).

The Seebohm Report was far from universally welcomed by child welfare professionals, appearing to herald the end of specialist work of mental health and children's officers, but it signalled a clear policy intent based on views about the causation of social problems and thus about what should be their remedy. The following extract from a speech in the House of Lords by Conservative life peer Baroness Brooke of Ystradfellte (Hansard 29 January 1969 vol 298 cc1168-93)[3] captures the ambitions of the reform agenda supported cross party. Services were to be delivered to whole families, accessibly based in neighbourhoods and democratically accountable to local government. Central control from Whitehall was deemed unnecessary and even dysfunctional:

> [W]hat the Seebohm Committee want is that these different services shall be amalgamated into one. They want this for the sake of every household: not only the families with children, but the childless couples, and individuals, often old people living on their own. As the family or household is one, so they maintain that the social services designed to meet its needs should be one ... I think there is compelling force in the decision of the Committee to recommend that this new, unified family social service should be the responsibility of the local authorities. They are much nearer to the family needs and requirements than some remote area-based board selected and directed from Whitehall could possibly be. We want personal decisions and actions taken by committee members and officers and field workers who live on the spot, or near enough to it to be in touch. We want to avoid long-range examination of impersonal paper problems, and instead to have human contacts which will convey the human's needs.

A similar vocabulary can be found in the 1983 Barclay Report, on the roles and tasks of social workers in England and Wales, which argued for more emphasis on community engagement, with social workers based in locality teams acting as brokers of resources.

The social services departments advocated by the Seebohm Report were established in 1971, but by then the political mood had shifted.

---

[3] http://hansard.millbanksystems.com/lords/1969/jan/29/social-services-the-seebohm-report.

The economic crises of the 1970s brought a fascination with, and faith in, markets. The consensus was shattered. Excessive public spending and perverse incentives created by welfare were deemed responsible for Britain's relative economic decline. The fascination with economic liberalism and market competition flourished on both sides of the Atlantic under Margaret Thatcher and Ronald Reagan. Morally, personal responsibility, not mutual dependency, was the order of the day. Efficiency in public services, achieved through improved performance and value for money, was the new priority. This version of efficiency needed quantity. It needed things to measure. It needed to know 'what works'.

1980: Can social work survive? The 'what works?' question surfaces

Social work was particularly singled out for reproach. Its deficits, critics alleged, were amplified by its location in the recently created social services departments. Brewer and Lait (1980) were trenchant in their criticism, arguing that the Seebohm Committee had 'made up its mind before it looked at the evidence', and it had been dominated by a 'phalanx of social workers, or more precisely social work teachers' (p 22). The authors lamented the lack of representation of the medical profession (Brewer was a doctor) on the Committee and argued that the establishment of social services departments had severed the relationship between doctors and social workers and had allowed an anti-professional, politicised version of social work to blossom with no proper knowledge base:

> [D]octors occasionally show themselves to be capable of attaining precisely defined objectives. Social workers would be hard put to it [sic] to demonstrate comparable precision of objective or attainment, except perhaps in fostering or adoption, or more negatively in removing children from bad homes or placing unwanted old people in institutions. (p 39)

For these activities, they suggested, a good dose of common sense would do, but Brewer and Lait also made a strong case for evidence-based methods. The woolly psychodynamic legacy was making social work ineffective, they argued. Short term, behaviourally oriented programmes were the answer; compassion unfettered by evidence was dangerous: 'In our experience, too many social workers seem to think that when science comes in at the door, compassion flies out of the window. We are all for compassion, but we believe that compassion which is applied without regard for its consequences is both misplaced and dangerous' (p 190).

Brewer and Lait's remedies are not entirely without merit. They had favourable things to say about locality-based teams and community development, but the take home message is that we need more science. They commended Brian Sheldon's Single Case Experimental Design, which stresses disciplined progressive hypothesisation, where social workers are clear about what they think is happening and go about testing this and their attempts to intervene empirically. Sheldon's view has been influential in spawning the evidence-based practice (EBP) movement in social work and some of the messages are important. However, as we shall see, the danger comes when other forms of knowledge are denounced and centuries of accumulated wisdom about the human condition ignored. In such a regime, doing the right thing becomes a quaint and slightly silly aspiration in need of a good evidenced-based shake-up. We will examine the presuppositions underpinning this worldview in more detail in due course.

Despite the maelstrom of criticism, the Seebohm departments were to remain for some years but an increasing preoccupation with risk to children and an escalating regime of performance management were to create the conditions for wholesale change in favour of specialisation and centralisation. There is an enduring moral tension between the rights of the many to freedom from scrutiny and the intrusive intervention of the state, and those of the relatively few who are dangerous or who come to serious harm at the hands of others. The precautionary principle is constantly in a discursive and moral dance with proportionality but for the last two decades this has been resolved in a particular direction. Bureaucracy has burgeoned to 'manage' the risk. Many more children die in road accidents than at the hands of their significant others, but we do not see a great deal of political or media scrutiny of road safety. Instead, terrible, but low-probability, deaths provoke intense scrutiny of systems and practices, with a focus on the prevention of false negatives (that is, avoiding missed cases) and an assumption that more referrals to children's social care will keep children safe. Thus, policy shifts inexorably towards the precautionary pole (see also Chapter eight for further discussion of the implications in terms of framing the stories told about protecting children).

Making the case replaces casework: the 1990s and the tyranny of risk

During the 1990s, a number of commentators argued that the discretion of social workers was being curtailed through intensification of formal monitoring, particularly by the courts, so that referrals were routinely processed in a 'legalistic' fashion, with a preoccupation with their forensic and evidential features. Parton summarised this as follows:

> In effect, the space occupied by social work between the state and the family is being refashioned such that professional discretion is being curtailed in some areas but extended in others ... If in the past child abuse has been seen as a medico-social problem, where the expertise of the doctor has been seen as focal, increasingly it has been seen as a socio-legal problem, where legal expertise takes pre-eminence. It is in this context that a pre-occupation with child protection takes on a new significance and the focus of social work with children and families emerges in a different form. (Parton, 1991: 18)

Thus, the assumptions hold sway that dangerous situations may be differentiated from safe ones; abnormal development from normal, good enough parenting from bad enough, urgent from routine. Assessment checklists were produced containing scientific knowledge stripped of equivocation, void of the sceptical scientific attitude. This then becomes the yardstick against which interventions are judged, by the courts, by senior managers, by the inspectorates, by the 'complaints' system, and so forth. This formal rationality is inextricably linked to the rise of child protection (White, 1998).

With the inquiry reports into the death of Jasmine Beckford (London Borough of Brent, 1985), Tyra Henry (London Borough of Lambeth, 1987) and Kimberley Carlile (London Borough of Greenwich, 1987), the late 1980s saw the rise of 'scientific' risk assessment. Social workers were criticised for failing to recognise the (retrospectively obvious) 'signs and symptoms' of abuse, and for concentrating instead on maintaining their relationship with parents. The report into the death of Tyra Henry stressed the importance of *preventing* danger, while the Beckford inquiry a few years earlier had insisted on the use of 'predictive techniques of dangerousness' (London Borough of Brent, 1985: 289).

The net effect of these inquiries was the reinforcement of the belief that such tragedies were preventable; the imperative was to perfect the criteria for sorting the dangerous from the others. Physicians, psychiatrists, psychologists and social work academics duly set about creating the taxonomy of dangerousness, which would help social workers and others to undertake 'scientific' assessments, hence avoiding the pitfalls of intuitive practice. Dale et al's (1986) treatise on 'dangerous families' was a product of this era and provided the organising framework for the Department of Health publication *Protecting Children: A Guide for Social Workers Undertaking a Comprehensive Assessment* (Department of Health (DoH), 1988), which was known colloquially as 'the orange book'. The original catalyst for the production of this guide had been a Social Services Inspectorate Report which had noted that detailed assessments, of the kind recommended by the Beckford Report were 'conspicuous by their absence' (London Borough of Brent, 1985: 12) in many of the authorities they visited. However, as Parton (1991) points out, it took the furore related to the Cleveland child sexual abuse scandal (1987) (in which social workers and paediatricians were criticised not for complacency, but for zealotry, to convince ministers of the urgent need for codified principles in child protection work.

Of course, once the essential ingredients of competent assessment had been identified, it became possible to create bureaucratic mechanisms to check whether they had been properly carried out. These procedures soon became ends in themselves, despite a growing recognition that dangerousness was, in fact, extraordinarily difficult to predict (Dingwall et al, 1983). Social work practice was subject to managerial and judicial scrutiny as though it were a straightforward process. So, if things went wrong, there must be a failure to follow procedures.

The 'orange book': the seductive certainties of standardised assessment

While giving a warning about the 'dangers' of checklists, the DoH (1988), asserted:

> Practitioners should be aware of the constellation of factors often associated with dangerous families ... Practitioners will be aware of the characteristics of the seriously immature personality which craves immediate gratification, has low tolerance, makes superficial relationships and has little concern for others ... However ... it is the quiet, over-inhibited person with a serious personality disorder whose dangerousness, in terms of exhibiting unexpected violence, is often unrecognised until too late. (p 12)

The guidance offered to the practitioner was aimed at the amelioration of this risk. The components of a comprehensive assessment were listed as follows: causes for concern; the child; family composition; individual profile of parents and carers; the couple relationship and family interactions; networks; finance; physical conditions; and summary. No area of parental experience was excluded from the gaze of the child welfare agencies, for example question 70 asked 'Can you remember being held by your mother or father to comfort you when you were a child?', while question 112 concerned the couple's sex life. There were 166 questions altogether, with further sub questions addressing specific aspects of 'family functioning'. Attachment theory figured strongly. Behaviours, as apparently diverse as 'experiencing problems with logical thinking' and 'having difficulty having fun', were presented as symptoms that may 'indicate lack of a normal, healthy attachment experience' (DoH, 1988: 43). Attachment theory had the capacity to act as an organisational lubricant, being sufficiently malleable to allow it to be invoked to justify any number of interventions. It remains thus in the present day as we shall see in later chapters.

From concern about dangerousness to concern about concern

During the early 1990s concern about the child protection process itself began to surface. The Children Act 1989 had, in any case, been drafted with a view to providing a remedy for both professional naiveté or incompetence and excessive zeal (Cleveland, and subsequently Orkney – see the 'Clyde' Report, 1992). It thus perpetuated the common law presupposition that parents *possess* moral *rights* in respect of their children, as well as *responsibilities* towards them.

A number of research studies (Thorpe, 1994; DoH, 1995a) had concluded that, although many children entered the child protection system, the vast majority were not placed on child protection registers – a pattern which endures, as we have noted already. Moreover, once the child protection investigation was complete, they were unlikely to receive 'family support' services, which were their proper entitlement under section 17 of the Children Act 1989:

> Although [local authority] policy statements indicate a range of children in need – from children suffering abuse or neglect to less critical concerns – ... it was apparent ... that social workers still regard 'children in need' as a separate category of children with a low priority rather than all the

children with whom they work. Many social workers have not yet made the intellectual shift away from categorising children according to services. Research suggests this may be why nearly half of child protection cases which did not reach a case conference received no services for support either. (Audit Commission 1994: 58)

The principle of 'partnership' with parents, which was central to the guidance and regulations issued after the implementation of the Children Act 1989, was hammered home, with practice guidance being issued on the 'challenge' of partnership in child protection (DoH, 1995b). While the *raison d'*être of this practice guide was the apparent *intrinsic* incompatibility between professional surveillance (with the implicit threat of coercive intervention) and 'partnership' with parents, an explicit message emerges – if social workers and managers follow these simple rules, the situation can be remedied. The 1988 *Protecting Children* guide, with its transparent discourse of dangerousness, remained the recommended format for 'comprehensive assessment'.

England: new public management, 'deliverology' and child protection

In the late 1990s, under New Labour, policy focus subtly shifted from the family to childhood vulnerability. Childhood moved to centre stage as a means to secure a positive and economically active future, to meet the challenges posed by increasing globalisation. While family forms diversified under a socially liberal state, 'parenting' became a very political concern and a major site for state intervention. In organisational child welfare terms, we see an important shift away from services that are framed primarily in terms of 'the family', to those that are explicitly 'child-centred'. Social services departments were reconfigured into children's services and technology became a key change agent, enabling the tracking of cases remotely by managers.

The Framework for Assessment of Children in Need and their Families (DOH, 2000) placed the child as the object of attention and intervention. The Green Paper *Every Child Matters* (Chief Secretary to the Treasury, 2003) stated the government's intention 'to put children at the heart of our policies, and to organise services around their needs' (p 9). A key unit of organisation became the individual child not the family. The state became child-centric:

However, the way in which the 'child-centric' systems have been developed and operationalised is based, almost exclusively, on an administratively determined psychologised view of children with little room for other voices and perspectives and little space for debate and negotiation ... In many ways the thinking behind the development sees children in very instrumental ways: as the objects of a variety of concerns which need to be acted on rather than agents of their own lives. In this respect, it is not just the 'family' and professional practice which has become fragmented, but children themselves. (Hall et al, 2010: 17–18)

The late 1990s and early 2000s also saw a series of reforms leading to highly centralised 'command and control' approaches to regulating the activities of social workers in child protection. Alongside a reformulation of the role of the welfare state, there was also a continuation from the Conservatives of what became known as 'the managerial partnership state' (Featherstone, 2004). Although there were differences from the foregoing Conservative agenda, New Labour's infatuation with the methods of private business was, if anything, stronger. Enabling, brokerage and regulating were emphasised over providing, and where the state did provide this was both targeted and subject to target setting. New Labour's approach to public administration provided the perfect medium for so-called new public management (NPM) to flourish (Dillow, 2007). Its ideological contours are that: a central elite know best; strong top-down management is the key to quality and performance; workers are self-interested and inefficient; the standardisation of processes and explicit targets drive quality and these are ensured by rigorous micromanagement using performance indicators (Chard and Ayre, 2010). In the context of human services and particularly child protection, NPM has been centrally concerned with managing institutional risk (Munro, 2009), creating a climate of 'targets and terror' (Bevan and Hood, 2006). It is impossible to understand the genesis of the reforms to child welfare in England without understanding the key policy mantras as outlined above. Moreover, they are proving very difficult to destabilise, despite a range of compelling critiques.

The reform of children's services was accelerated in 2000 with the death of Victoria Climbié (Laming, 2003), but, as we shall see from its unmistakable family resemblances, its progenitors are NPM and performance management. Victoria died in London as a result of long-standing cruelty at the hands of her great aunt and her partner.

Her death prompted a highly influential inquiry into professional and institutional failure. As a result, government put in place a series of reforms drawing heavily on concepts of 'business process management', electronically enacted through the Integrated Children's System (ICS) (Shaw et al, 2009; White et al, 2010). The ICS attempts to micro-manage practice through the imposition of a detailed, work-flow model of the case management process and other processes.

Many of Laming's broad diagnostics of the failures contributing to Victoria's death are accurate enough. However, his relative neglect of human, interactional and social factors means that the policy responses, particularly the standardised processes and 'information sharing' initiatives, have been based on a set of erroneous assumptions. The most notable of these is that catastrophic child deaths are substantially the result of professionals failing to record or share information. Such failures are not trivial, but in our view rarely are they causal. Rather, they are ubiquitous features of many cases that do not end catastrophically, as Wastell notes:

> [T]o be sure that this evidence is decisive, we need to know how often it was present in other cases but did not lead to calamity. ... Unless it can be shown ... that assessments, information gathering and multi-agency collaboration were conspicuously worse in the serious cases, how can it possibly be claimed that these were critical causal features? (Wastell, 2011: 11)

In England, the policies, implemented under New Labour were to result in a 'perfect storm': time scales, targets and the Integrated Children's System. It became apparent that a key casualty of these 'reforms' was time spent with families. The audit tail was well and truly wagging the practice dog. Rather than protecting against system failure, these factors exacerbated 'latent conditions for error' (Reason, 2000; White et al, 2010) because they made the work bureaucratically *complicated* while failing to take account of its human complexity.

The system reassessed

The death of Peter Connelly in 2007 provoked the establishment of a national 'Social Work Task Force'. The ICS, with its form-based artefacts and rigid processes, was marked out for urgent attention. Further scrutiny of the system followed the general election in 2010 with establishment of the Conservative–Liberal Democrat coalition.

Professor Eileen Munro was commissioned to scrutinise and advise on reducing bureaucratic burdens in children's services. She concluded:

> The demands of bureaucracy have reduced [social workers'] capacity to work directly with children, young people and families. Services have become so standardised that they do not provide the required range of responses to the variety of need that is presented. This review recommends a radical reduction in the amount of central prescription to help professionals move from a compliance culture to a learning culture ... (Munro, 2011: 6–7)

However, despite the introduction of a new vocabulary of discretion and professional judgement, the Munro Review does not appear to have resulted in a different dominant modus operandi. With some notable exceptions new public management and service complexity remains the order of the day.

Grounded in economic arguments from the 1980s onwards that marketisation leads to efficiency, competitive commissioning of provision has proliferated, leading to increased fragmentation of services (Carey, 2014). The promotion by successive governments of 'public service' markets focused on tendering, commissioning and measurable 'outcomes' brings with it enormous transaction costs and unhelpful and inappropriate vocabularies:

> Beneath the 'market interface' of competing for and awarding service contracts on 1–3 year cycles, the day-to-day language, design and delivery of social care practice has become profoundly shaped by commercial sales and business management disciplines – just as the architects of the 'internal market' had hoped. Service managers today, if they are to hope to 'win business', are encouraged to be able to define their product clearly; to have and to meet targets; to have data that proves their service product really 'works' (evidence of outcomes); to have done their market and competitor research; to know their unique selling point and have a perfected 'market pitch'... For many public and charitable professionals today, whether working in service delivery or as commissioners and spenders of public funds, the public service market orthodoxy is so deeply embedded into their working environment they may never

have experienced, or be able to imagine, a different way of organising and delivering public services. (Evans, 2016: 22)

This kind of management thinking has an iron grip – when things don't work, people must try harder, objectives must be 'smarter', measures must be more 'measurable'. A gigantic amount of waste is thus generated, which sucks in ever greater proportions of the shrinking budgets of all services – those who deliver and those who commission. It is an incorrigible position since the solution to 'failure' is always doing more of the wrong thing (Caulkin, 2016). In this system, failure is ultimately inevitable. The public services market does not operate like a commercial market – prices are not set by demand, rather through competitive tendering they move inexorably downwards to the point where providers can no longer provide (Evans, 2016). 'Everything we know about management is wrong. Force-fitting humanity's crooked timber into the clean right angles of a mathematical abstraction is a recipe for failure' (Caulkin, 2016: 33).

To complicate matters further, welfare provision has undergone further fragmentation through increasing specialisation. There is an increasing tendency for services to be functionally specialised and they are typically 'parsed' into short-term and long-term teams, or subject to criteria based on chronological age, or legal status (Seddon, 2008; White et al, 2015). A key feature of the post Climbié reforms was the distinction drawn between initial and core assessments, with separate and rigid time scales imposed on each. This was a further hammer blow to patch-based working, advocated in the Seebohm and Barclay reports, as it incentivised centralised teams where the time scales could more efficiently be monitored. It also led to the establishment of a range of other specialist teams, meaning families routinely, and as part of normal practice, are passed from one team and one worker to another.

These mindsets have resulted in reductive provisions that have generated new risks for families experiencing multiple difficulties (Carey, 2014, Baldwin, 2009). Despite the rhetoric of integration and information sharing, disintegration of the professional work with families is more typically the case. This, coupled with a strong moral narrative of prevention through early intervention, has produced some disturbing developments in the system. At a time when public services are shrinking, this chapter, alongside Chapter one, has detailed an extraordinary escalation in compulsory intervention into family life. There is no money, but, somehow, this intervention makes economic sense. If we are to understand how this has happened and why it seems such a potent force internationally we need to examine some of its legitimating narratives. We attend to these in the next chapter where we consider the rise of prevention science and the quest to rewrite social deprivation in bodies and brains.

Concluding remarks

This chapter has taken a broad sweep, setting the scene for understanding the contemporary lived experiences of families as explored in Chapter four, where despite, or indeed because, of a panoply of effort at a range of levels, families experience multiple difficulties and indeed risks in accessing help for their troubles. It documents how and why practices have become fragmented and sets the scene for the rise of prevention science which we now turn to explore in the next chapter.

THREE

Building better people: policy aspirations and family life

Introduction

> Sympathy requires an important intellectual and emotional bond between people far apart in space and time. Our biological age has reopened questions about the nature of this bond. (Fuller, 2006: 119)

> [A] human mind needs the rest of its body, suitable surroundings and a full memory of past activities if it is to think and act. And it needs them every bit as badly as it needs its brain. (Midgley, 2014: 53)

In the previous chapter, we described the forces that coalesced to support the current dominant modus operandi in child protection and welfare. We argued that models of risk and predictability have converged with the international rise of bureaucratic managerialism and centralised state control of local provision through the regulation and inspection of marketised services. These factors have created the conditions for a moral settlement to take a firm hold. This is characterised by a residual, but strongly legitimised, role for the state in preventing damage to children, which carries high levels of opprobrium for those parents seen as failing to optimise their child's developmental potential. The idea that childhood experiences are important and can be formative clearly has a common-sense truth to it and obviously traumatic experiences in childhood will have lasting impacts. However, a vocabulary has emerged in which notions of toxic parenting and the quest for optimum developmental flourishing create new mandates for the state to act. We argue that these are necessary to explain the sharp rises in national rates of child removal, and particularly permanent removal of very small children documented over the last decade. They also contribute to service fragmentation by privileging intervention in the early years in the form of 'evidence-based' parenting programmes.

Rewriting social deprivation in bodies and brains: the great leap backwards

> The learned debate about the nature of inequality in class and ethnically stratified societies is a spurious controversy. All major positions, ranging from biological determinism associated with conservative ideologies to environmentalism linked with liberal politics, are actually rationalizations for the status quo of intergroup relations. One key underlying idea shared among seemingly opposed experts is that the position of the oppressed stems from their own weaknesses. (Valentine et al, 1975: 117)

For centuries, there have been debates about whether the causation of deviance, 'abnormal' development and social inequality and disadvantage could be found in biology, inadequate or deficient parenting, society, culture or chance. A seminal paper, written in 1975 by anthropologists Valentine and Valentine (Valentine et al, 1975), critiques the theory of 'socio-genic brain damage' put forward by a distinguished anthropologist Ashley Montegu. Montegu was a progressive thinker attempting to identify ways by which the state could 'cure' social disadvantage and deprivation. In the US these communities were disproportionately African American.

Montagu's argument is summarised as follows:

> Social malnourishment, both structurally and functionally can be just as brain/mind damaging as physical malnourishment … it constitutes an epidemic problem of major proportions … it can only be solved by those improvement s in the environment which will assure any new-born baby the realization of his birth right, which is the development of his potentialities to the optimum. (Montagu, 1972: 1058, cited in Valentine et al, 1975)

In a forensic critique, Valentine et al draw on the considerable evidence from cultural anthropology to argue that the human organism develops normally under astonishingly different, and often very challenging, environmental conditions. They caution against extrapolating from studies charting the organic effects of non-stimulating environments in the brains of laboratory animals, and point to the adaptive nature of many of the behavioural traits of the poor who are being pathologised by bourgeois commentators of both conservative and liberal persuasions. 'A consensus has been developing that low-status groups suffer from organic damage and dysfunction of the central nervous system. This consensus is approaching orthodoxy with the construction of theoretical formulations such as Montagu's "sociogenic brain damage"' (Valentine et al, 1975: 117).

So, genetic determinism (through 'bad genes') and theories of environmental intergenerational disadvantage, associated respectively with conservative and liberal commentators, ultimately lead in the same direction: namely, surveillance and interference in the lives of some communities, frequently with little, or highly conditional, real help. 'Despite enormous amounts of data and highly elaborate specialised technical procedures, the experts are conspicuously failing to integrate available information and knowledge into useful insights' (Valentine et al, 1975: 130). This argument, taking place nearly half a century ago, showed extraordinary prescience.

In 2015, Adam Perkins, a neurobiologist of personality, wrote *The Welfare Trait: How State Benefits Affect Personality*, arguing:

> [C]hildhood disadvantage has been shown in randomised controlled experiments – the gold standard of scientific proof – to promote the formation of an aggressive, antisocial and rule breaking personality profile that impairs occupational and social adjustment during adulthood ... A welfare state that increases the number of children born into disadvantaged households therefore risks increasing the number of citizens who develop an aggressive, antisocial and rule-breaking personality profile due to being exposed to disadvantage during childhood. (2015: 2–3)

In support of this bold thesis, Perkins marshals a series of supporting artefacts, the randomised controlled trial, a version of neuroscience disseminated through the Harvard Centre on the Developing Child, mouse genetics and the equations of the economist James Heckman. Perkins provides a florid example of the contemporary mindset, but his key ingredients are noteworthy and becoming ubiquitous. They legitimise a policy shift away from income maintenance and support and towards residualism and surveillance.

The idea of the infant brain damaged by neglect is a key contemporary leitmotif. Since the 1970s, when the Valentines' powerful arguments against the theory of socio-economic brain damage took place, there has been an explosion of brain science and it is now exerting a potent influence on mainstream policy. There is an emphasis on promoting 'targeted early intervention' to improve the lives of disadvantaged children, recast as those suffering from Adverse Childhood Experiences (ACEs). Sociogenic brain damage is back in the entrancing detail of fMRI (functional Magnetic Resonance Imagery) images. The promise of social improvement by optimising the development of the infant brain is popular across the political spectrum. It can solve the problem of unequal life chances; it can fix people for good.

The report of the 'First 1001 Days All (UK) Parliamentary Working Group', entitled 'Building Great Britons' (2015), could have been penned at any point in the last hundred years or so:

> Society prospers, and is an enriching environment in which to live, according to the nature of its citizens. The more citizens are physically and mentally healthy, well educated, empathic, prosocial, hard-working and contributing to the costs of society, the better society will flourish. As there is a rise in the proportion of citizens who are damaged, physically or mentally ill, poor at relationships, antisocial, violent or criminal in their behaviour, and placing a drain on society's resources, so the quality of society worsens. In the UK today there are too many citizens in the latter category. (pp 13–14)

The report goes on: 'We do not blame – they are to a large extent the product of their childhoods as, in turn, were their parents and grandparents. We do propose that decisive action be taken to ensure the proportion of good citizens rises sharply in the future' (p 14). The infant brain makes an early appearance in the report, with an emphasis on (sociogenic) 'damage' and irreversibility:

> Just as a positive environment can support optimal development for babies, so too can a negative environment disrupt development, with potentially lifelong damaging effects on the developing brain which can predispose to mental health problems, risk-taking behaviour, depression, anxiety and even violence throughout the lifespan. (p 8)

This is just one example in a gamut of policy aimed at early intervention and the amelioration of social disadvantage and its damaging sequelae. The invocation of brain science in the contemporary UK policy context can be traced to the US and the so-called 'decade of the brain' launched by George Bush in 1990; its aim was to enhance citizens' knowledge of the benefits to be derived from brain research.

Rose (2010) traces the arrival of brain science on this side of the Atlantic to an agenda passionately promoted by Iain Duncan Smith, a former leader of the Conservative Party, and his ally from the Labour Party, Graham Allen MP, noting 'the structure of the developing infant brain is a crucial factor in the creation (or not) of violent tendencies' (Allen and Duncan Smith, 2009: 57). Thus, in this neo-phrenological argument, criminality is depicted as hardwired in the brain. Vigorous supportive campaigning from child welfare activists ensued. In 2010 another Labour MP, Frank Field, entered the fray. Again, the aspiration was to end poverty and disadvantage, with the infant brain as a primary change agent. The allusion to stunted brains in the text below is to the work of Bruce Perry, whose brain images are now famous for their sketchy lineage:

> The development of a baby's brain is affected by the attachment to their parents and analysis of neglected children's brains has shown that their brain growth is significantly reduced. Where babies are often left to cry, their cortisol levels are increased and this can lead to a permanent increase in stress hormones later in life, which can impact on mental health. Supporting parents during this difficult transition period is crucial to improving outcomes for young children. (Field, 2010: 43)

One of Perry's earlier works is entitled 'Incubated in Terror' (1997), which rather speaks for itself. This campaigning, in due course, resulted in the establishment of the Early Intervention Foundation in 2013, a recommendation of the reports by Graham Allen (2011a, 2011b), which make extensive use of neuroscientific arguments (for an extended critique see Wastell and White, 2012, 2017), with multiple references to the Harvard Center.

That the Harvard Center has been so influential should not surprise us unduly. The aspirations of this impressive cross-disciplinary project were to produce a translation of the primary science, aiming to create a public sense of shared responsibility for children and for strategic investment in their future. The tone is communitarian not totalitarian. Nevertheless, the production of a 'core story' required the development of a new metaphorical vocabulary. The processes by which this was achieved were complex, drawing on anthropology, cognitive science and linguistics to map 'conceptual models' in public use, synthesising these with expert knowledge to develop 'powerful frame cues' (Shonkoff and Bales, 2011: 20) in the form of metaphors and values. Expert knowledge was thus recast through folk understandings, so to show people what they think they already know; of course, domestic abuse is a bad thing, it damages children's brains. The act of translation by the FrameWorks collaboration, in the US context, involved challenging a dominant cultural notion that childhood adversity was something to be overcome by rugged self-reliance (Bales, 2004). This, by necessity, had to involve stoking up the 'damage' and 'toxicity' of suboptimal childhoods. The stage was thus set for the 'core story' to inform policy, not least at the more coercive end of the state apparatus. But this core story is just that. It is a simplified take away version of a complex and contested field where most the work is on animals and extreme clinical populations. The Harvard version of neuroscience does not resemble neuroscience itself but it has been extraordinarily influential, as we might expect after all this effort, and as we explore below. The FrameWorks Institute has more recently collaborated with the NSPCC, Big Lottery, a Better Start Initiative and the Dartington Social Research Unit to create and evaluate a core framing story about the impact of ACEs. This builds on the 'toxicity' metaphors from the Harvard partnership. While there are some hopeful and helpful aspects to the ACE narratives, which invoke 'buffers' to toxicity in the form of relationships with adults, it has profoundly pathologising potential as well. We can see the contrasting ways in which ACEs can be invoked in the following two quotations. The first talks about strengthening families; in the second, from a local authority website, we can see the net-widening potential of the concept as almost half the population are pulled into the 'suboptimal', toxic childhood category. People are encouraged to work out their ACE scores to inform themselves of the risks of developing a range of nasty sequelae from diabetes to criminality. Is the news that one is biologically broken likely to be received well? What has happened to the sociological notions about the impact of labelling and self-fulfilling prophesies?

> The presence of caring adults and stable environments are a necessary component for a child's healthy development and for building resilience. Safe, stable, nurturing relationships between children and their parents or caregivers act as a buffer against the effects of toxic stress and other ACEs. In fact, research is now showing that the presence of supportive relationships is more critical than the absence of ACEs in promoting well-being. If parents are struggling, other

adults – like teachers or coaches – can be present to provide the safe, stable, nurturing relationships that a child needs. We can also invest in supports and promote policies that strengthen families and set them up for future success. (p 11) http://onecaringadult.co/wp-content/uploads/2016/08/ Facilitators-Guide.pdf

The term Adverse Childhood Experiences (ACEs) is used to describe a wide range of stressful or traumatic experiences that children can be exposed to whilst growing up. ACEs range from experiences that directly harm a child (such as suffering physical, verbal or sexual abuse, and physical or emotional neglect) to those that affect the environment in which a child grows up (including parental separation, domestic violence, mental illness, alcohol abuse, drug use or incarceration). A Blackburn with Darwen study found that almost half (47%) of adults across the Borough have suffered at least one ACE, with 12% of adults in Blackburn with Darwen having suffered four or more ACEs. The study has shown that the more ACEs individuals experience in childhood, the greater their risk of a wide range of health-harming behaviours and diseases as an adult … ACEs can therefore have a negative impact on development in childhood and this can in turn give rise to harmful behaviours, social issues and health problems in adulthood. There is now a great deal of research demonstrating that ACEs can negatively affect lifelong mental and physical health by disrupting brain and organ development and by damaging the body's system for defending against diseases. The more ACEs a child experiences, the greater the chance of health and/or social problems in later life. https://www. blackburn.gov.uk/Pages/aces.aspx

In Chapter eight, we explore not only how using framing techniques can help us deconstruct the devices used to persuade, but whether they hold possibilities for us to advance our concerns and win hearts and minds. Our point here is that storytelling matters. The strategy of the Harvard Center and its collaborators has been spectacularly successful, precisely because it has been able to 'shout science' and produce a version of development which can merge easily with a technical vocabulary of calculation, targeting and risk. Whatever its intentions it has had a range of effects which now require different vocabularies of challenge.

An 'evidenced-based review' commissioned by the UK government to guide judgement in child protection cases, argues without equivocation:

> A baby's stress response system is unstable and reactive; it will produce high levels of cortisol if the baby's needs are not being met, or if the baby is in an environment which is aggressive or hostile. Persistent and unrelieved chronic stress in infancy results in the baby's brain being flooded by cortisol for prolonged periods. This can have a toxic effect on the developing brain, with detrimental consequences for future health and behaviour. (Brown and Ward, 2013: 44)

Centres of expertise, such as the Harvard Center, operate at the interface between the world of science and the realm of policy and practice. Their expertise, however, is communication and persuasion. The project has been very effective in persuading senior politicians, practitioners and civil servants. Although the scientific credentials may be questionable (Wastell and White, 2012), the Allen Report, for instance, ultimately led to the establishment of the Early Intervention Foundation, which exerts considerable influence on UK policy and practice. This charity's strap line is RIGHT FOR CHILDREN, BETTER FOR THE ECONOMY.

The remit of the Early Intervention Foundation is broader than brains, with significant use made of economic arguments. We are witnessing the rise and rise of 'prevention science', the bold ambitions of which seem to dominate even the most apparently benign shifts in policy and practice discourses. For example, work showing the impact on women of the removal by the state of successive, multiple children (Broadhurst et al, 2015a), shows signs of being translated into a new category, 'repeat removals', with offers of help to mothers potentially conditional on them 'consenting' to the use of long-acting reversal contraception, now, or for the time being at least, deemed medically safe (Broadhurst et al, 2015b). Prevention science builds on the models and logics of epidemiology but blends these with claims to predictive validity through careful targeting. Parental life style and choice make their appearance as relevant variables in developmental risk. The trajectory of current policy is increasingly towards 'policing' of women's pregnant bodies on the one hand, 'positioning poor mothers as architects of their children's deprivation' (Edwards et al, 2015: 167), and intensified state surveillance over family life on the other (Lowe et al, 2015).

Prevention science and human perfectibility

Thus, the late 20th and early 21st centuries have seen the steady rise of 'prevention science'. Its aim is to stop damage in its tracks, so to ensure *optimal* human flourishing. An early paper sets out the goals as follows:

> The goal of prevention science is to prevent or moderate major human dysfunctions. An important corollary of this goal is to eliminate or mitigate the causes of disorder. Preventive efforts occur, by definition, before illness is fully manifested, so prevention research is focused primarily on the systematic study of potential precursors of dysfunction or health, called risk factors, or protective factors respectively. (Coie et al, 1993: 1013)

The keystones of prevention science are: risk, with its associated probabilistic reasoning; the notion that variance is a form of 'illness'; a preoccupation with identifying underlying causes; ensuring efficacy and cost-effectiveness with rigorous methods; and translation of the scientific findings for an audience of policy actors. 'Whatever national program for prevention research is developed, it must ultimately be translated into practical applications that will "sell" in schools, hospitals, playgrounds, homes, clinics, industries, and community agencies nationwide' (Coie et al, 1993: 1020).

Early intervention usually means early childhood intervention based on indicators of risk. Thus 'targeting' becomes another hallmark of the paradigm. Prevention science is not concerned with mass immunisation, or fluoridation of the water supply. It is behavioural 'dysfunctions' and 'diseases' it seeks to nip in the bud. Problems, such as socio-economic disadvantage, which are less malleable must be rewritten as something else: 'Variables that are hypothesized to be relatively non-malleable but that have major significance for the development of psychopathology, such as heredity, social class, or gender, should be translated into constructs that are susceptible to influence by interventions' (Coie et al, 1993: 1020).

Prevention science incorporates the familiar tenets of developmentalism, but these are combined with mathematical economic modelling, behavioural economics and a particular version of evidence-based practice, which in turn allows the generation of 'effect sizes' to plug back into economic models and so on.

At this point we will focus on the specific economic and scientific arguments which are at play in the context of policy using the UK as our main example. We take the following features of prevention science in turn and examine the presuppositions and myths that support them. First, we explore the economic modelling which has legitimated the targeting of particular forms of intervention. As it is core to the modelling we then revisit developmentalism and the idea that early years are foundational to the development of normality and deviance. The preferred method of ameliorating risk is though targeted programmes which must be subject to robust evaluation. The public accountability for spending on prevention, particularly in the US context where universal provision is scarce, relies on certain mandated form of evaluation and evidence – the state and benefactors will only pay for 'what works' and only some methods will provide the 'effect sizes' the economists need. It has proved a very attractive export.

The economists seize control

Policy in the US since the late 1990s, and increasingly in the UK, has relied heavily on economic models of investment in human capital. The work of the economist James Heckman has been dominant and the elision of mathematical modelling, child development and brain science forms the hallmark of his work. Introducing their modelling, Cunha, Heckman and Schennach (2010) describe how their 'multistage technology' maps developmental stages in the child's life cycle and estimates 'substitution parameters that determine the importance of early parental investment for subsequent lifetime achievement' (Cunha et al, 2010: 884). The economic modelling is complex, and claims to predictive validity are strong. It is very attractive to policy makers as it promises a rigorous scientific basis to guide public investment. The published paper (Cunha et al, 2010) is 50 pages long (with a further 50 pages of supplementary information) and is dense with mathematical equations and esoteric economic terminology (for a detailed critique see Wastell and White, 2017).

As with brain images, there is an obvious concern that policy makers (and practitioners) are seduced by the vocabulary and the equations, and thus they do not raise key questions. Considering more of Heckman's research, poverty is not part of the 'equation' as the following quotation shows from a widely cited earlier paper:

The widely discussed correlation between parental income in the child's college-going years and child college participation arises only because it is lifetime resources that affect college readiness and college-going … . Job training programs targeted at the disadvantaged do not produce high rates of return and fail to lift participants out of poverty … these programs are largely ineffective and cannot remedy the skill deficits accumulated over a lifetime of neglect. (Heckman and Masterov, 2007: 475)

Instead of poverty, Heckman prefers to invoke biology: 'a particular variant of the monoamine oxidase A gene, which has been associated with antisocial behaviour and higher crime rates is triggered by growing up in a harsh or abusive environment' (Heckman, 2013: 16).

On adverse child environments (typically described as associated with unwed, single-parent, teenage, or uneducated mothers) Heckman and Masterov (2007) note that the reality of lone parenting is a far cry from media depictions of celebrity lifestyle-choice single parenthood. Instead it is associated with 'many pathologies' (p 463). The solution is for mothers to try harder: 'Controlling for maternal ability, never-wed mothers who provide above average cognitive stimulation to their children can largely offset the circumstance of single parenthood in terms of their child's cognitive outcomes' (p 466). This seems to lead policy to a preoccupation with targeted parenting programmes.

The underlying neuroscientific and educational models for Heckman and his colleagues are in fact quite limited (see Heckman, 2013). They are based primarily on three US studies, the Abecedarian, Perry and Chicago projects, which provided home-based educational interventions to young infants. These all yielded promising short-term results on children's cognitive and non-cognitive development, but were small scale and often evaluated by people very committed to the projects themselves. They also relied on notions of critical periods and the importance of the first three years leading to a 'cliff edge' at the end of the intervention periods, so it is unsurprising that results could be difficult to replicate at 24-month and 36-month follow-up periods. Bruer (1999) provides a seminal critique of these interventions, of their underlying assumptions and limited long-term, or even medium-term benefits. Heckman also cites the Family Nurse Partnership as an example of an efficacious intervention, although again the evidence for sustainable benefits is equivocal. In a follow-up study when children reached the age of 12, David Olds, the originator of the programme, reports enhanced partner relationships and 'mastery', and less 'role impairment', but no effects on the mother's marriage, relationship with the biological father, intimate partner violence, alcohol and other drug use, arrests, incarceration, psychological distress or reports of foster care placements (Olds et al, 2010). These disappointing results may well be the unintended consequences of concentrating resources on the first three years and then slamming the service door.

Heckman also draws heavily on popularised versions of neuroscience from the work of Bruce Perry, whose brain images have proved a ubiquitous feature of policy on both sides of the Atlantic and as we have noted are featured in major UK government reports and evidence syntheses (Allen, 2011a, 2011b, Brown and Ward, 2013).

Preferred responses: infant determinism, parenting and programmes

The persistent preoccupation with the preventive potency of the early years has led to the proliferation of particular types of intervention. The review of the evidence for these programmes undertaken for the UK Early Intervention Foundation (Dartington Social Research Unit et al, 2015) reviews over 100 programmes, 32 in depth. These are variously aimed at improving attachment and maternal sensitivity, social and emotional skills and behaviour, and language and communication. The overview report concludes: 'We recommend that Early Help services delivered through children's centres and other sites draw more heavily on programmes and practice with a strong evidence base and that there is an improved focus on monitoring outcomes' (p 13). This is not a particularly surprising recommendation given the proliferation of 'early (childhood) interventions' all with uncontroversial aims of improving things that are good for children. Twenty years into the prevention science paradigm, there is little firm ground offered to people who commission services but they will certainly be expected to spend money on outcome-focused evaluations of the programmes they have bought, regardless of their existing evidence-based credentials. Evaluations have a long history of equivocation with a search for ever more sophisticated methodological purity accompanying each caveat.

Substantial chunks of the prevention science paradigm rely on the promises of rigorous randomised controlled trials to assess efficacy against a set of outcomes. But, what counts as an outcome? Who decides what a 'key measure' is? At what point in time do we measure 'change'? How long do families get 'on the programme', before their 'outcomes' are measured? Tunstill and Blewett (2015) dub this 'outcomes theology', noting its effect on policy and practice. Thus, as Pearce et al (2015: 6) note:

> To be sure, randomised trials can offer a counter-weight to unwarranted certainty or decision-making that rests on a narrow set of assumptions drawn from previous experience or personal bias. But judgments must still be made about the nature of the question a trial is meant to address (could it be asking the 'wrong' question?) and about the role of potential bias in interpreting the evidence generated (what assumptions have been made and could they be contested?). This is the paradox of randomised trial evidence: it opens up expert judgment to scrutiny, but this scrutiny in turn requires further expertise.

Randomised Controlled Trials (RCTs) do not neutralise political choices.

Having somewhere to go and someone to talk to are ubiquitous features of most 'interventions'. So, why is it that researchers persist in paring down 'interventions' so bound up in the communicative practices of people and so self-evidently laden with contingent social meanings and matters of relationship and trust, to a set of 'ingredients', ostensibly separable from their medium of transmission? Under the current policy regime 'demonstrating effectiveness' has become essential to securing and sustaining funding and funding is increasingly targeted. Targeting has become a branch of prevention science of considerable complexity and ambition in which biological markers are beginning to play a role.

Implementation science: targeting and intervention efficacy

Acknowledging the variability in outcome measures for young children experiencing preventive interventions, Barlow and Axford argue:

> Problems in demonstrating benefits are not evidence, as some have argued ... of the weakness of the research about the importance of early parenting. Rather, they reflect a continuing lack of the type of nuanced information about what works, for whom, under what circumstances ... that is necessary to ensure that services are effective in meeting the needs of parents experiencing significant adversity. The lack

of success in changing outcomes also highlights the need for better use of the rapidly developing 'implementation science' that enables both practitioners and policy makers to deliver services with integrity, and in ways that match parents' needs and their readiness for change. (Barlow and Axford, 2014: http://www.emeraldinsight.com/doi/full/10.1108/JCS-04-2014-0025)

Implementation science steps into prevention to offer a possible 'cure' for the problems of generalisability. It seeks to address why the effects of 'evidence-based' programmes sometimes wane over time and may have unintended effects when applied in a new setting. It also promises to provide economies of scale by combining compatible interventions in particular sites for targeted populations. Implementation science shares the same vocabularies as prevention, hence it perpetuates its vexing paradoxes.

Like prevention science, implementation is taking a biological turn. In an editorial of a special edition of the journal *Development and Psychopathology* addressing 'what works for whom', Belsky and Van Ijzendoorn (2015) discuss the importance of focusing on the 'genetic makeup' of those receiving interventions as potential determinants, or moderators, of their efficacy. It is worth following the argument as it is likely to be illustrative of the direction of travel. We have already mentioned the built-in costs of the prevention science paradigm but for Belsky and Van Ijzendoorn this may be resolved by considering variation in susceptibility to an intervention. This, they argue, may provide the arguments necessary to persuade policy makers that they really are getting more bounce for the ounce. More effective genetic and epigenetic targeting is the way forward.

Despite the difficulty in finding the elusive 'genetic modulator', there are signs that biomarkers will play an increasing role in future implementation science. The uncritical identification of 'biological' with 'objective' is the hallmark of the contemporary zeitgeist. Leaving this aside, using genetic susceptibility to argue that only certain children should get high-quality foster care, or any other sought-after service, because it 'won't work' for others raises major ethical issues. Indeed, we might argue, it shows the potential futility of this form of reasoning. However, Belsky and Van Ijzendoorn argue: '... this should not lead to ignoring replicated evidence that some individuals are more open to environmentally induced changed, for better and for worse, due to their genetic makeup' (2015: 1).

Where might this logic take us? It can only drive us in the direction of more screening. It produces the notion of 'a new "human kind": the susceptible individual' (Rose, 2010: 23) and potentially a great deal of surveillance in the name of producing better people. Surveillance has already become normalised. But not all citizens are equal:

> Welfare recipients ... are more vulnerable to surveillance ... Persistent stereotypes of poor women, especially women of color, as inherently suspicious, fraudulent, and wasteful provide ideological support for invasive welfare programs that track their financial and social behavior. [These] communities are more likely to be the site of biometric data collection ... because they have less political power to resist it. (Eubanks, cited in Giroux, 2014: 130–1)

We note the invocation by Belsky and Van Ijzendoorn of the potential of the burgeoning field of epigenetics to open up new avenues of research and policy: 'future work will hopefully extend research of this kind to determine whether ... epigenetic processes are a critical pathway by which intervention effects become instantiated' (2015: 4).

Epigenetics: friend or foe?

Biologically uniting nature and nurture, epigenetics promises a great deal. It has joined with prevention science and is playing an increasing role in the policy and practice debates about what is best for families and what constitutes good parenting. Where might the emerging fascination take us?

The last decades have thus seen a profound shift in our understanding of biological processes and life itself. At the heart of neurobiology's ascendancy is a paradox, described by Rose and Rose thus: '[Biological] discourses are at once essentialist and Promethean; they see human nature as fixed, while at the same time offering to transform human life through the real and imagined power of the biotechnosciences' (2012: 24). Whereas genetics has conventionally focused on examining the DNA sequence (the genotype), the burgeoning field of epigenetics examines additional mechanisms for modifying gene expression in manifest behaviours, physical features, health status and so on (the phenotype). It provides a conduit mediating the interaction of the environment on an otherwise immutable DNA blueprint, and invites a natural interest in the impact of adverse conditions, such as deprivation or 'suboptimal' parenting. In brief, a number of epigenetic mechanisms have been identified, integral to the functional biology of multi-cellular organisms, such as those which maintain cell differentiation and prevent your liver from becoming your heart over time. For our purposes here, we mention the two 'celebrities' of the literature which have received most attention in prevention science: DNA Methylation and histone modification. Both of these can change gene expression – in the popular argot – by 'switching genes on or off'. Both work on the gene transcription sites (where RNA [ribonucleic acid] is produced for protein synthesis) with methylation dampening responsiveness and histone modification either augmenting or diminishing it. The implications for social policy of this plastic biology are far reaching.

Discoveries at the molecular level are fuelling the aspirations of the Developmental Origins of Health and Disease (DOHaD) paradigm. In 2015 the International DOHaD Society launched its manifesto. Again, economics and productivity feature strongly in the narrative.

> Harmful environments during early development may cause failure to achieve full physical and mental potential, and a loss of human capital … Moreover, an unhealthy lifestyle in prospective parents … passes greater risk of NCDs [non-communicable diseases] to the next generation. This perpetuates cycles of poor health, reduced productivity and shorter life expectancy, trapping populations in a trough of low human capital from which they cannot easily escape. (International Society for DOHaD, 2015: 1)

Under the spotlight are individual 'choices' – unhealthy eating, lack of exercise, smoking and alcohol use and wider environmental exposure to microbes or toxins. Increasingly, though, psychological 'stress' is being implicated in epigenetic changes. The manifesto goes on to list the following aims:

> Support optimal timing of pregnancy, healthy weight, good macro- and micronutrient status, physical activity, sleep and other behaviours in women and their partners before, during and after pregnancy …. Promote positive maternal mental health and reduce rates of untreated depression and anxiety in pregnancy …. Support breastfeeding, healthy complementary feeding, regular physical activity, a healthy lifestyle and parenting skills, to exploit critical windows of opportunity for the optimal physical. (International Society for DOHaD, 2015: 1)

The goal of epigenetic optimisation carries many moral and ethical implications. There is a clear focus on reproduction and maternal behaviours. Women's partners are mentioned only once – they too must eat and sleep well and undertake physical activity. There is nothing modest about these policy aspirations, though it is noteworthy that there is no explicit reference to the alleviation of poverty and social disadvantage.

The molecular level might be very helpful in understanding the mechanisms giving rise to cancer and might equally further our understandings of the impacts of toxins or infectious agents. Things are murkier when policy is focused on behavioural changes on the precautionary principle that a variety of quite ordinary 'choices' might be damaging the epigenome for the next and even subsequent generations.

The UK Houses of Parliament briefing on epigenetics and health stresses the need to equip practitioners with the competencies and skills needed to support behaviour change: 'Evidence from epigenetics research is [that] epigenetic changes are potentially modifiable through lifestyle and diet. Advice to pregnant women on behaviour change to avoid exposure to potentially harmful factors during early embryonic development is likely to be particularly important' (Houses of Parliament, 2013: 4). Thus, the implications of the 'biology of social adversity' (Boyce et al, 2012: 17143) are profound. 'Hard' heredity, in which genes were fixed for life (insulated from environmental influences, life chances and choices) drove the eugenics movement of the late nineteenth and early twentieth centuries. In its extreme form, the 'barbarous utopia' of the Nazis (Meloni, 2016: 28) made biology politically unacceptable. Epigenetics shows every sign of making biology political and moral again. As Meloni notes, freeing us from the determinacy of our genetic inheritance might help make the case for more resources to 'fix' or prevent damage to the epigenome of disadvantaged groups, but it may also have less desirable sequelae:

> This all sounds desirable, but how likely is it in a society where class, race, and gender inequalities remain so vast? What is our society going to make of the notion that … the socially disadvantaged are also (epi)genetically damaged? … And what will oppressed groups do with this flurry of epigenetic studies concerning their own condition? (Meloni, 2016: 221)

Significantly absent from many of the otherwise sophisticated discussions about the potential uses of epigenetic understandings is the proper response of the state to those who refuse to comply with actions deemed to be in their own best interests, or in the interests of their future offspring. Yet, these are thorny matters indeed as Rothstein et al (2009) note:

> [E]pigenetics raises difficult questions about the obligations of society to preserve the soundness of the human genome and epigenome for the benefit of future generations. In developing a principle of intergenerational equity for the human genome and epigenome, optimum social policy lies between indifference to the health burdens of future generations and eugenic notions of manipulating heredity to improve the human condition. (p 27)

As we have noted, current developments in biotechnology are not historically unique. They form part of an enduring project to 'fix' people, which has, in its various guises, both liberal and conservative valences, but which tends to lead policy and professional reasoning in particular directions. Prevention and targeting are prominent motifs in an increasingly residual and conditional welfare settlement, providing a natural slot for technologies which can claim to tease out individual susceptibilities. Rather than challenging orthodoxies, both neuroscience and epigenetics at present appear to be being used to support old moral arguments, regardless of what the scientists might anticipate among themselves. As Kahn (2010: 311) notes: '[S]cience is not an anthropomorphic being, it does not "tell" anything. Scientific data has no meaning until one interprets it and such interpretations are inevitably packed with qualitative judgements.'

At present the moral mood music seems to take us into the inhospitable womb. Studies on 'foetal programming' by adverse 'maternal mood' burgeon, drawing much inspiration from laboratory work on rats. An initial trawl on Google Scholar yields 30,000 hits for foetal programming. This is a field of frenetic scientific activity. Again, much of this work is on laboratory rats in highly controlled and manipulated environments. Work on human populations following extreme famine and natural disaster show scientifically interesting effects but overall are quite reassuring about the resilience of our species. Given the range of environments in which human beings have thrived for millennia, we must ask ourselves why the preoccupation with stress in utero, where the infant not the mother is the focus of expert concern, and where does this activity lead us as a society?

Epigenetic thinking is Janus faced, as Mansfield and Guthman (2014) note. It breaks out of the straitjacket of genetic determinism – we are molecularly free. We are porous, we absorb, we interact. These understandings may inform fights for social justice, add a punch to arguments for compensation following exposure to environmental chemicals, show how oppression gets under the skin. But all this plasticity has an ugly side: 'The notion of optimization renders epigenetic changes as disorderly, as damage not adaptation …. things once normal, in a statistical sense, can become abnormal, in the sense of not-optimal' (pp 3 and 11).

Gestation becomes the playground for epigenetic manipulations. Women are responsible for optimising good biological influences, making the right choices, consuming the remedies and therapies on offer to 'optimise' their uterine environments. We thus come perilously close to losing the category 'normal'. This is a paradox because epigenetics is about difference and inevitable variation in response to the outside world, but by equating difference with disease through the notion of suboptimal conditions it creates a particularly potent form of eugenic thinking. In the US this is heavily racialised as Mansfield and Guthman note. This side of the Atlantic this modus operandi is almost certainly going to be refracted through social class.

'Optimisation' of early life environments and the conflation of 'suboptimal' with 'marginal maltreatment' might make the case for benignly intended public health and parenting education approaches (Barlow and Calam, 2011), but they also erode the 'normal' and expose particular sections of the population to increased scrutiny in the name of prevention. We can see harbingers of what might be on the way. There are epidemiological studies linking fathers' lifestyle (smoking, diet) to disease risk in the male line (Pembrey et al, 2006), and arguments from developmental biologists in favour of broad-ranging public health or environmental interventions.

> [T]here is compelling evidence that the male germline is also vulnerable to environmental impacts which confer substantial health risks on offspring. The clear implication of these findings is that effective mitigation of environmental health risks is unlikely to be achieved by sex, or life-stage-specific behavior change, but will require action that recognizes the much greater breadth of these risks across the life course. (Cunliffe, 2015: 67)

Nevertheless, developments in the policy world support Mansfield and Guthman's arguments. It is mothers who will bear the brunt of the current epigenetic line of reasoning.

Biologically uniting nature and nurture, epigenetics promises a great deal and is delivering crucial new understandings of disease, but it joins with prevention and implementation science to reconfigure relationships between parents, children and the state. The difficulties in accessing biological samples from the brains of human subjects has led to a search for reliable markers in peripheral tissues as proxies for changes in the central nervous system. A current favourite is cheek (buccal) cells. The relatively uninvasive nature of such tests opens up the population to epigenetic screening.

This form of argument has proved attractive to the Early Intervention Foundation (EIF). On 12 April 2016, its second annual conference took place, and included a session addressing 'What can genetics tell us about the possibilities of early intervention?' It is noteworthy that this was sponsored by the Economic and Social Research Council – the major UK government social scientific funder. The discussion is summarised on the EIF website[4] by Duncan Tessier, Assistant Director of Early Intervention & Prevention, Children's Services, Barnet Council:

> The session started with Professor Leon Feinstein posing a big question: we know that around £17bn per annum of government spending focuses on the dealing with the financial costs of 'late intervention' – such as family breakdown, mental health and domestic violence services. But what percentage of that £17bn is actually preventable in a (theoretical) world where we got early intervention 'exactly right'? Part of the answer could in turn depend on the extent to which genetics determines outcomes. If poor outcomes are pre-determined by our genes, then might that limit the effectiveness of early intervention?

This is heredity back with a confident 21st-century makeover. In a bizarre pincer movement deadly to the provision of ordinary help, the notion of plasticity, recast as perfectibility, and hardwired genetic taints are back. It is transparently a version of neo-eugenic thinking and crucially, these biological arguments are only necessary if policy

---

[4]   http://www.eif.org.uk/reflections-from-eifnatcon-what-can-genetics-tell-us-about-the-possibilities-of-early-intervention/ last accessed 28/2/17

makers are trying to fight off the moral arguments that people need to live decent lives with adequate resources.

Concluding remarks

This chapter argues that, increasingly, doing the right thing is replaced with fixing the right people. Complex and abstract vocabularies of risk, science, evidence and economics have been melded together to deliver increasingly persuasive stories that apparently beguile policy makers and appear to be very compelling for practitioners. Who can possibly want a vulnerable baby's brain to be damaged beyond repair by our lack of early and resolute intervention? However, we ask policy makers to consider whether disadvantage would be acceptable if the genes and brains bore the insult unscarred. We argue strongly in this book against this but do need to consider whether we are shouting into the wind. Are all the policy cards ACEs?

FOUR

Family experiences of care and protection services: the good, the bad and the hopeful

Being unable to tell your story is a living death, and sometimes a literal one. If no one listens when you say your ex-husband is trying to kill you, if no one believes you when you say you are in pain, if no one hears you when you say *help*, if you don't dare say *help*, if you have been trained not to bother people by saying *help* (Solnit, 2017: 19, emphasis in original).

Introduction

Stories of pain, hurt, betrayal and violence are told to professionals everyday and, indeed, are heard by them often as they struggle with huge caseloads and worries of their own at home and at work. However, a key theme of this book, and central to its mission, is a concern that the language and theoretical and practice tools available to them are impoverished and increasingly inadequate. This is partly due to contemporary challenges in terms of funding of course. We have already highlighted how those services and families who need the most have had the most taken away since 2010. But it is also due to the inadequacy of a model that translates need to risk routinely, colonises a variety of sorrows and troubles within a child protection frame, and has abandoned or lost a sense of the contexts, economic and social, in which so many are living lives of quiet, or not so quiet, desperation.

This chapter brings some of these lives into sharp relief. It has two purposes in the context of this book: first to shine a light on lived realities but second to offer some really vivid examples of how we might begin the process of designing services *with* families rather than *for* them. Thus it acts as an essential bridge to the subsequent chapters where a social model is fleshed out across policy and practice contexts.

The chapter draws on a number of studies conducted by the authors, in particular a detailed study of families and their experiences of welfare services, hereafter referred to as Study One (Morris et al, 2018b) and an enquiry on the role of the social worker in adoption, ethics and human rights (Study Two), which explored the perspectives of birth families, adoptive parents and adopted young people (Featherstone et al, 2018).

Background

It is worth dwelling a little on how we arrive at such studies, whose voices shape the research agendas and how the guiding questions are influenced. In some strands of social work and social care, active participation by those using services has become established. That is not to say that co-construction is the norm but there have been significant strides in disability studies and mental health studies (see, for example, Beresford and Carr, 2012).

The picture in child welfare is best described as uneven. Certain voices are more, or less, in evidence and there are complex, interlinking constraints at play. For some, a real sense of shame prevents participation, with fears about being judged and found wanting inhibiting contributions. For others, the sense of a lack of legitimacy or a respected space to contribute means their voices are absent. The conversion of need to risk ensures a harsh reality for families; by being positioned as risky their voices are marginalised and the processes of shame and stigma silence possible contributions. Scrambler (2018, no page no.) argues this is the weaponsing of stigma: 'a political strategy of heaping blame on shame'.

As we noted in the Introduction, this is complex territory: underdog or underclass discourses and good family/bad professional binaries are extremely unhelpful in terms of understanding or engaging with lived realities. Children's circumstances are complex, with often competing strengths and problems. Movements towards inclusion of children, families and communities in research cannot afford to sanctify 'the family' and deny the harmful experiences that exist within families and communities. But, without serious attempts towards processes of co-construction of the research agenda, it is difficult to see how policy and practice development can build on children's lived experiences and the priorities of families and communities.

In Study One the researchers attempted to find ways of supporting those who were the focus of the studies to shape the design and analysis and in Study Two imaginative means were sought to bring diverse and often conflicting voices together to reflect on complex ethical and human rights issues. We draw from these not only to demonstrate the need for change, but also to highlight the seeds of more hopeful possibilities, particularly in relation to co-production, that go well beyond research developments.

The following themes emerged to varying extents in accounts from families and young people.

Negotiating help in the shadow of risk

There were many examples provided by birth parents of feeling powerless in a climate that was seen as very risk averse. Birth mothers reported high levels of domestic abuse and suggested they were being punished for having a violent partner and/or having experienced domestic abuse in childhood. In such contexts the risk of future emotional harm was the category frequently used by the system, and was seen as a particularly unjust basis for permanent separation. As we indicated in the Introduction, being able to tell a story of where you have come from and how you understand your present and future is essential to resilience. Unfortunately, we found many birth mothers who considered their stories of seeking to survive in very frightening circumstances were colonised by professionals and returned to them in a shape that was experienced as unjust and shameful. For example, the use of the term 'failing to protect' was considered as particularly cruel when women were living in fear and where indeed contradictory imperatives were imposed by public and private law. For example, contact with violent ex-partners was instructed to happen within one set of legal proceedings, whereas public law expectations were that children should not be exposed to violence.

Being judged and stigmatised simply for having a history of care and/ or abuse was an issue for birth parents in Study Two. Care proceedings, involving new-born babies, were identified as being particularly traumatic, with a lack of attention, in particular, to the impact on the mother of having just given birth. Residential settings were described as being too often focused on monitoring risk rather than providing help or therapeutic support. Contact centres were often grim, forbidding places with bars on the windows. Women with disabilities highlighted the disabling environments in which assessments were carried out.

Fear of an unsympathetic and punitive response was seen as inhibiting families from asking for help when it was needed. Parents with mental and physical health problems and learning difficulties all reported concerns about asking for help because of the emphasis on risk. They reported receiving an assessment rather than support and feeling they were being scrutinised rather than helped.

Some of the adoptive parents' experiences echoed those of birth parents when requests for help were viewed through the prism of risk and they were constructed as 'the problem' by social workers. For example, adoptive parents' requests for help could result in their being considered to be failing to protect their children. Their strategies to manage a child being bullied at school, for example removing the child from the school, could result in such a response.

Moreover families described seeking help but instead repeatedly getting an assessment, investigation or, in some circumstances a far more extensive service than they envisaged: "By seeking help, I made things worse." "Over assessment is really stressful ... it raises your hopes – you can spend a whole week managing the assessments." Endless assessment visits to the home could be deeply frustrating, and indeed harmful, especially when these involved children who might associate professional visits with traumatic earlier episodes of removal.

Fragmented roles and services

The definition of the social worker role as being 'the social worker for the child' was a source of concern as it often led to a lack of support for parents and carers but also led to fragmented services: "Children are part of families – a social worker cannot only be the child's social worker" (birth mother).

Chapter three described the backdrop to a complex and bewildering tapestry of services. Seeking help was often the start of a difficult and, at times, traumatic journey around and through services. Families that sought help (rather than those who had services imposed) rarely knew what was needed initially, but knew they were struggling and tried various services and agencies. "… also, because some people haven't got a clue and have not been in that situation before, so they don't understand where they need to go or what they need to ask …". The conditionality attached to receiving help proved a stumbling block for many families. They regularly described what were experienced as hurdles to accessing help (Were they living in the right place? Did they have the right referral? Had they got the right diagnosis?) Rarely, if ever, were families able to describe initial points of contact that simply asked the family to talk about their needs and then dealt with any inter-agency matters 'behind the scenes'.

> 'How the hell did I manage to get my daughter the help in the first place? It was so bloody difficult. It was a total nightmare and I think that is the thing that all of us keep

coming back to. I know the system, I have worked within the system, and it practically destroyed me.'

Once some form of help was secured families had a common experience of the help (whatever it might be) being conditional on them complying with preset requirements. These included attendance at clinical appointments, signing agreements specifying certain domestic arrangements or behaviours, attending particular classes or courses. At times such requirements made accessing the help almost impossible, or limited its value. Agencies also imposed rigid conditions on the provision of help (this included the length of time certain help could be offered, the age(s) at which it could be provided, standard start and finish dates and lengths of time on waiting lists). Those that approached their work with families differently, with few conditions and limits were greatly valued:

> 'They are brilliant with me; they have got all the time in the world. Sometimes you go in and if you have had a core group thing and you're a bit upset and that, she will take to you to one side. The liaison officer ... She has never not got time for you. Do you know what I mean? She will say to me, "I know where you are coming from, I know how you feel". She is really good.'

Experiences of being helped were not the same as receiving a service, and this was often an important distinction drawn by respondents.

> 'We felt it was a bit pointless, but because it was the only help on offer, we sort of persevered with it. They have got a very good reputation, so we persevered with it. There was nothing else coming up. I had a big thing in my head about not wanting us to be labels. I quite liked the idea, he has got attachment difficulties, he is adopted. It was an explanation you could give to people for his crazy behaviour. Do you know what I mean?'

Help sometimes came from everyday sources, with professionals (such as youth workers and head teachers) coming to the aid of the family in ways that were underappreciated:

> 'I think in terms of engaging parents, he is a brilliant Head, and that does filter down to a lot of his staff as well. I think

the management was really good. That was our stability amongst everything else that was absolutely chaotic … If that hadn't been there, my daughter wouldn't be alive today.'

Money and practical resources matter

Financial concerns formed a common thread within the family narratives in Study One and practical needs were highlighted in Study Two.

The data concerned with finances can be grouped into two sub themes, and these are not mutually exclusive:

1. Family concerns about how their own resources and funding limited their capacity to work with services. This was often reflected in accounts about the costs of accessing services (examples included travel, missed work) or the ways in which they (the family) felt that they could not meet the needs of vulnerable family members (examples included day care, house moves).
2. Family recognition of the restrictions on services and the finite nature of many services and resources (for example discussions about cuts to early help and informal support, concerns about worker caseloads).

There is common ground between these two stands of financial concerns. Family narratives recognised both the limits set by their own finances and the limits set by the funding of services. Families rarely held individual workers responsible for the limited resources of their services, however they described considerable frustration when service arrangements failed adequately to reflect the limits to their own family finances. Appointments with therapeutic or clinical services were commonly given as examples of help being offered, but in such a way families struggled to access the help. Clinics that were held out of the area and appointments in working hours when jobs were precarious were cited as points of frustration, and at times despair.

Birth families in Study Two highlighted the importance of social workers providing practical help and the constraints placed on their capacity to care because of issues such as poverty and poor housing.

Time

Temporal concerns ran through all the family narratives and could be loosely grouped into three themes:

Time-limited services: the use of targeted services for brief periods (often six to eight weeks) provoked consistently negative responses. If such services were experienced as helpful, families needed longer to embed the change, and felt abandoned. If the service had not had the anticipated impact, frustration developed about inadequate time to achieve change. None of the family case studies included family accounts that explained or justified short-term interventions, suggesting systemic problems with explaining and managing with families preset time-limited services.

Timelines for interventions: professional narratives about avoiding delay infused family accounts of some services, often in child protection and care. Families felt rushed and prematurely judged, arguing that, in some circumstances, professionals had arrived at final decisions before any meaningful work was completed with them.

> 'But I was quite happy to do all the courses they advised me to, but I couldn't physically finish them in time, as they wanted me to. When we finished court, they told me before I was having supervised contact with XXX, they wanted me to do a course that didn't exist. They wanted to do a Freedom Part 2 course and it doesn't exist. I phoned one day, I phoned three different Women's Aids in the area. Every single one said it doesn't exist.'

Time spent waiting for services: repeatedly families talked about meeting the criteria for a service (which can be a difficult process) and then finding that they had to join a waiting list, even when needs were acute. But there were also interminable waits once services commenced, with families recounting stories of hours of waiting in receptions, in wards, in police stations. Nothing productive was felt to occur while waiting, rather it was considered that it eroded confidence, cooperation and tolerance:

> 'We were watching her fall to pieces in front of our eyes, no one would do anything until she was sectioned ...
>
> You then wait hours, for A&E to get somebody, a consultant psychiatrist to see you. There you are, feeling suicidal, and you are there for about 24 hours, often. No bed offered; you are on a chair, and you are waiting to be seen by a consultant psychiatrist. Consultant psychiatrist comes to see you and then confirms that you have to be hospitalised. You then have to go into a children's ward ...

You then have to wait in the children's general ward until a psychiatrist from the paediatric team, that is, CAMHS. The consultant on duty comes to see you to assess what they think should happen to you. That whole process is traumatising for a young person ... The staff were lovely, but the whole process and the waiting was just horrid.'

When this experience of categorisation was overlaid by the application of formal interventions that were not negotiated the families' experiences became particularly chaotic: "Could have tipped us over the edge, with her coming in and out, bailiffs at the door, it were all just too much, too much." Indeed, for at least one family, services became considered as 'toxic' as multiple services came and went in a bewildering and traumatising fashion.

Cold-hearted encounters

'She saw me sobbing in reception and she walked past me twice and then said there were nothing wrong.'

'I said to the social worker I wasn't prepared to leave because XXX was being sick, he was alone and somebody needed to be with him. But it seemed that nobody wanted to listen to what we had to say. ... It was horrible. All I wanted to do was hug him and I couldn't hug him, I had to sort of hold him here because he was covered in sick; his clothes were covered in sick. It was crusted where they had not changed his clothes.'

The large number of accounts of cold-hearted encounters suggests a need to pay attention to interpersonal skills and humane practices. In many cases humane practice may not have changed the outcome but may have reduced the level of antipathy generated and ensured families did at least feel they mattered to some extent.

'I don't feel like she had any time for us at all. I didn't feel like she wanted to listen, she had made her mind up before she had even got here. I think the thing is, because XXX's dad has got a history of drug use and prison, she formed an opinion before she met me. I have never taken drugs and have never been in prison. What happened was she came into the meeting, a child in need meeting at school, and me and (my partner) had an argument. She sat there and said, "I was driving here today in the car and I was thinking, 'shall I put this on child protection or shall I just kick it out? No, I think I will put it on child protection'". That is exactly how she said it, in front of all the other people. I thought, "How can you make that judgement on one …?" She met me once. Then she has made a judgement coming to work in her car. That put me off her straight away.'

The gap felt by families between their highly charged, emotional experiences and detached, and what were seen as dismissive, professional responses, compounded difficulties and reinforced a sense that their feelings were unworthy of recognition. Such experiences of engaging with services resulted in families assigning emotive and emotional labels to agencies ('cold', 'stand offy' 'jobsworth') that permeated the families' use of the services. On occasions careless practice caused long-term problems, exacerbating already difficult situations: "They released her sedated after midnight without letting anyone know, she got attacked trying to get home, staggering around with the tablets and we didn't know."

Relationships matter

The narratives included accounts where professionals had sought to clarify with the families exactly what occurred, and more importantly what feelings were provoked. Where practitioners did seek to work reflectively with the family and established shared understandings of their encounters, family members recounted being able to invest more actively in the working relationship.

Repeatedly, across the range of family members, the importance of the relationship that was developed with a social worker was stressed.

Birth family members gave accounts of both poor and good relationships. They related experiences of feeling deceived by social workers whom they considered had not been honest with them. They described not understanding or being helped to understand why their child(ren) were permanently removed; being unfairly judged/labelled ("the report said I was 'hostile' so he could not stay, but I was not hostile – I am 'loud'" – birth grandmother from a traveller background); and generally being treated in what they perceived were inhumane ways.

Birth family members emphasised the importance of social workers listening to their views, being respectful and honest, recognising strengths and displaying acts of kindness. It was considered that the nature of the relationship could influence what happened with the child. Examples were given of differing outcomes for children in the same family (that is, adoption or remaining with the parents) and these were, at least in part, attributed to the quality of the relationship with the individual social worker. It was considered vital that social workers have the time to get to know and work with the family in non-judgemental ways.

Many of the responses from adoptive parents repeated the themes found in the birth parents' accounts. The relationship between the social worker and adoptive parents was considered to be key, with the importance of professional but caring social workers highlighted. Adoptive parents and adopted people also spoke about the importance of good communication, honesty, being listened to and being treated as an individual human being.

Key messages for social workers from a group of young adopted people were clear:

- Listen and don't judge.
- Be honest and don't lie about history.
- Be caring and friendly and fun.
- Get to know the individual.
- Get the right balance between being available but not too intrusive – work with the child/young person and give them choice.
- Help young people express their emotions and access support, but also it is important young people are not labelled and assumed to have emotional problems.
- Make young people aware of their rights and any changes to policy or legislation (for example, access to information).

Overall, the young people stressed the importance of social workers building effective relationships, getting to know the individual and giving them choice. Their support needs must be addressed, but they should not be pathologised because they are adopted. Instead their strengths need to be recognised and their resilience promoted.

The need to focus on practice in these conditions, arguing that by adopting particular theories/practice models social workers can begin to engage families in a more respectful and purposeful manner, has been stressed by many researchers and practitioners. And indeed, there is evidence to suggest that families identify and appreciate a change in practice tone and feel better able to work collaboratively with practitioners as a result (Laird et al, 2017a).

As the evidence in this book highlights there are serious limitations in relying on changes to practices to effect widespread systematic changes in children's life chances. But, however slight the influence on population level patterns, it is clear that families carry with them the hope offered by humane encounters and the hurt created by careless professional responses.

The deficit model of feedback

The ethos underpinning the Children Act 1989 was that of partnership. It promoted a permissive and supportive approach to family inclusion, reflecting a principle of engagement with family strengths and a movement away from families as objects of treatment and intervention. The studies above suggest, however, that services and processes are infused with an emphasis on deficits. This is a contradiction at the heart of service design and planning; partnership rests on respect and mutuality, but our current service design and processes are preoccupied with what doesn't work, what risk must be avoided and how to best manage failure. The role of families in feeding back on services offers a particularly useful illustration.

For the families participating in Study One the only means routinely open to them to express their views and offer their input into service and practice development was through putting in a complaint. There was rarely an opportunity to contribute through feedback, or participate in service design and commissioning. One local authority did offer a service user forum that some family members had attended, and valued greatly, but routine involvement was largely absent.

Critical to understanding the experience of engagement are family accounts of any challenge being labelled as problematic behaviour:

> 'So all the positive work that has happened up until now, the positive relationship I had with them has now, because my son is not talking to me, and I have taken it upon myself, to challenge the fact that everything is okay and I am saying I don't think it is. I am suddenly the problem again.'

> 'Their lack of communication was dreadful. I tried to get hold of the manager for about four weeks and I phone one week and say, "Can I speak to XXX" "Sorry, she is not in the office, I will get her to call you back". A couple of days go by, I phone back again, the same thing, consecutively, a good couple of weeks and then it was a long haul over

Christmas, where I phoned before Christmas and after into the new year, when everything had died down, still nothing back. Then I get this other worker phoning on behalf of XXX, and it wasn't even (my child's) worker. I wanted to make a complaint. She tried to resolve it and shush me over the phone. "You don't need to make a complaint now, I hope we can resolve this, because we do not need any further complications, by a complaint." I thought, "Well, I will go to the meeting on Monday and if I am not happy, I will make a complaint".'

The level of distrust was such that families told the researchers that professionals sabotaged plans when they had either been challenged, or directed to change, as a result of complaints. Families recounted episodes where they argued courts had made plans but social workers had deviated from these, or Family Group Conference plans had been poorly supported. The sense that the services pulled together to exclude them, as a punitive response to their complaints, was evident: "The court had said she [the Independent Reviewing Officer] wasn't to work with them, she was to be independent but they might have well skipped down the path together, going off for lunch giggling to each other."Whether the basis for these accounts is accurate or partial is, to some degree, a secondary issue. The key issue is how such levels of mistrust are generated and sustained, and the use of a complaints process as the only feedback mechanism offers an almost perfect example of processes that compound rather than alleviate the challenges of working together.

Navigating these complex service systems over a prolonged period of time meant families had developed a refined set of skills in understanding eligibility criteria, advocating for their services and managing multiple interventions. Some families were also aware that not all families could utilise the skills and resources necessary: "It's alright for me, I'm not being rude but I am intelligent and can read all this stuff, make sense of it, I'm feisty and can take them on. You've got no chance if you can't do these things."

Was partnership a wolf in sheep's clothing?

As indicated, the ethos of working together to achieve better outcomes for children underpins the Children Act 1989 and families could, and did, offer examples of tenacious and respectful working relationships that gave them a voice and role in supporting change:

'I found them incredibly supportive. I think they go above and beyond everything that is required of them really; they go out of their way to help you and support you, and they also help family members. So when I went to them when XXX left home, they helped me kit her new house out. They took the children away when we weren't able to. They don't look at you as an individual, they look at you, they look at the package that comes with you, they look at the circumstances and they go above and beyond what they need to do to help you. They are probably the best service that I have ever worked with.'

But reviews of the literature and studies of family experiences repeatedly suggest that the model of partnership envisaged by those involved in the Children Act has failed to come to fruition (Broadhurst and Holt, 2010). Indeed, we have seen the use of legislation and guidance, which was intended to be supportive, to achieve enforced cooperation. Families that 'failed' to work in partnership (for example, evidenced routinely through the use of written agreements that were not maintained) found their behaviours were subsequently used as a signal of their resistance and non-cooperation. But, as the family narratives in this chapter demonstrate, systems and services generate frustration and non-compliance by their very design.

'How the hell did I manage to get my daughter the help in the first place? It was so bloody difficult. It was a total nightmare and I think that is the thing that all of us keep coming back to. I know the system, I have worked within the system, and it practically destroyed me.'

The family case studies in Study One are rich accounts of how systems unwittingly, and wittingly, turn complex needs into complicated difficulties/risks. As feared by some, at the introduction of the 1989 Act, partnership has been a rarely attainable goal within existing child protection processes and services. But its use as a measure of the extent of family (or more often parental) resistance has been troubling. In essence, by placing an expectation of partnership on the table but implementing systems and services that caused, at the very least, some confusion and frustration, behaviour by families was inevitably found wanting. In a paradoxical development, levels of compliance became evidence of a family's commitment to partnership working, and debates emerged about 'authoritative practice' and the need to compensate for too generous a view of family potential (Tuc, 2012).

In the context of a risk-saturated child protection system, too often families recounted being asked to work positively with services that were not accessible, useful or relevant and they carried great anxiety about any non-compliance being used to judge them (even when taking up a service was too difficult).

That a failure to work in partnership could become the measure for the need for formal intervention merits careful attention. If, as the research we have explored suggests, family pathways through provision are ones of complex navigation, measurements, citing partnership capacity, are largely irrelevant. Indeed, system survival as a measure might indicate high levels of family resilience and resourcefulness.

Green shoots?

As we set out in the Introduction to this book, the capacity of our existing approaches to protect children, to translate need into risk, has profound and far-reaching consequences for families. This chapter has explored the evidence that, by the time families reach the service they need, their experiences of the welfare systems are such that needs have become acute crises and repeated risk-focused assessments have raised deep fears and mistrust. There is little in the family accounts that would suggest we currently have fertile ground for growing meaningful partnerships between families and services/professionals. However, there are glimmers in the family accounts of hopeful possibilities, and in this conclusion, it is worth dwelling on these.

First, families have built up an unparalleled knowledge of the range of welfare systems and services, and well-honed navigation skills. As this chapter illustrates, there are few opportunities to share these positively and productively. Obvious future possibilities present themselves. These can include peer support, co-construction of services, co-commissioning, or joint service evaluation, to name but a few. However, as those engaged in shifting cultures and practices towards more humane collaborative approaches know, even with the best of intentions the existing system design and culture hamper progress. For example, Leeds, a large UK authority, sought to embed family decision making in their child protection and care services and invested significantly. The evaluation of this programme shows real progress but also enduring limitations in the reach of changes within the current child protection paradigm (Sen et al, 2018). But noting the potential here is important: the skills and the knowledge held by families can be utilised through a process of co-production to arrive at transformative approaches that function at the levels of practice, service design and policy and internationally examples have emerged that offer rich learning.

Families also gain skills in dealing with substantive issues, for example parenting in difficult conditions or surviving and recovering from harmful encounters. For many this knowledge is painfully accrued but invaluable:

> 'At first, you just think it is all dangerous. At first, you think you have got to find him. You never find him, the police never find him; nobody finds him. It is real practical … You have to keep adjusting what you are doing. We have licked it virtually, the running now. That has been successful, with the help of XXX but also with our own knowledge. Your own knowledge builds up. That is another thing that agencies need to understand, is that parents build up knowledge of what they are doing as well, so that you get to use every day things differently.'

As other chapters make clear, the negative positioning of families as 'toxic' results in professionals fearing that collaboration with families will compound harm. Yet, studies and projects in the US and elsewhere have demonstrated that, in fact, peer support can support sustain change and reduce harm (see Chapters five and six).

In the studies some families had used social media to access other families and experienced both helpful and unhelpful responses.

> 'I joined everything when XXX was in care, because I needed to understand this, because I have never had this before. There were a couple of sites I removed myself off because there were nasty comments. They were going to court and writing "stop forced adoption". Grow up, you don't save your children if that is the way you are going to behave. Then there were a couple of people I ended up making friends with.'

Overall the use of social media was not widely commented on, but this may be a product of the timing of the research, or it may be that families are reluctant to declare and discuss this aspect of their experiences.

Ultimately, the analysis of family accounts reveals the value of encounters that engage with the everyday. For many families the distance between their everyday and the professionals' understanding of this was simply too great. There were poignant moments in Study One where this distance was painfully revealed. As part of the study, families provided photographs of images that represented their experiences. One included a sliver of a view of a garden (just a part of a garden toy and the surrounding grass). For this family, this is how professionals viewed their everyday, with so much out of focus or missing. For professionals, organisational cultures and local narratives about neighbourhoods may form barriers to such engagement. Our research into social workers' responses to poverty suggested that some social workers have incorporated an 'underclass' discourse in their descriptions of the communities and families they serve (Morris et al, 2018a). But for the families, the professionals that took stock of their everyday lives and used this knowledge to frame their responses were positively welcomed.

Concluding remarks

It is easy to become disheartened when exploring the experiences of families enmeshed in child welfare systems, and anxious for children and families who need, but fail to receive, sustained help. The experiences of families may be painful to hear and read but they also offer valuable insights into how different approaches could be built and supported. For families to become a source of wisdom and expertise about system design and best practice can seem a far-removed possibility within the current child protection project. But, by recognising the potential we begin to introduce hope into our working relationships, and a critical building block in the process of change.

FIVE

A social model for protecting children: changing our thinking?

> There can be no question that family case workers are in an exceptional position to make valuable observations on family life at first hand where they are protected, as they should be, from too large a case-load, and where they have had the kind of theoretical training in social science and practical training in social work which supplies them with the necessary background. 'The interplay,' says Professor Park, 'of the attractions, tensions, and accommodations of personalities in the intimate bonds of family life have up to the present found no concrete description or adequate analysis in sociological inquiry.' (Richmond, 1922: 227–8)

There is an irony in our resurrection of the *social* in social work. Mary Richmond, an early 20th-century social work pioneer, had in mind that social workers could make important contributions to social science. It is noteworthy that she quotes the sociologist Robert Park to argue that social workers might fill a gap which sociology had left open. Indeed, Richmond is widely seen as making a major contribution to the Chicago School of Sociology, with its emphasis on the ethnographic study of everyday lives. We would like to suggest that much may be gained by resuscitating the social dimensions of child protection practice, in order to nurture humane practice, through thorough understandings of the lives in the living, and also to inform with social science the 'evidence base' for policy and system design.

As we have noted previously, other areas of practice (than child protection) have much more clearly, in recent decades, highlighted the importance of the social and have been helpful to our thinking. In particular the 'social model' has challenged thinking across a range of fields, including disability and mental health. It has provided a philosophy and framework for articulating practices that challenge dominant biomedical models and their narrow focus on individual impairments, disease and risk. It has drawn attention to the economic, environmental and cultural barriers faced by people with differing levels of (dis)ability and built on a movement where those needing services were instrumental in articulating their rights to full participation in service design.

In this chapter we discuss the evolution of the social model in areas such as disability and mental health. In these domains, there has been a very clear 'other' to which the social model was responding – medicine and the notion of biological damage. In our view, similar individualised and pathologised stories are dominating thinking about child protection. It is thus timely to discuss our understanding of the possibilities presented by the notion of a social model for protecting children. We then turn to exploring more fully the key interrelated elements (as set out in the Introduction) of our reworking of a social model:

• understanding and tackling root causes;
• rethinking the role of the state;
• developing relationship(s)-based practice and co-production;
• embedding a dialogic approach to ethics and human rights in policy and practice.

Building on the discussions in this chapter, the next chapter then draws together some approaches to practice that we consider helpful in terms of future directions.

The social model of disability and its evolution

The social model of disability has its roots in the struggle of disabled people for the realisation of their civil rights. It was developed in the 1970s by activists in the Union of the Physically Impaired Against Segregation (UPIAS) and academics such as Finkelstein (1980), Barnes (1991) and Oliver (1983, 1990). It was called the 'Big Idea' of the British disability movement (Hasler, 1993) and has been effective politically in building the social movement of disabled people, with some notable successes such as the campaign for the Disability Discrimination Act 1995 (now part of the Equality Act 2010).

In the broadest sense, the social model of disability is about a focus on the economic, environmental and cultural barriers encountered by people who are viewed by others as having some sort of impairment – whether physical, mental or intellectual. The barriers disabled people encounter include inaccessible education systems and working environments, inadequate disability benefits, discriminatory health and social support services, inaccessible transport, houses and public buildings and amenities, and the devaluing of disabled people through negative images in the media.

If the barriers to full participation are not intrinsic to the individual but rather are social in nature, it is a matter of social justice that these barriers should be dismantled (Oliver and Barnes, 1998). Provisions necessary to meet the needs of people with impairments are demanded as a matter of right, rather than being handed out as charity to supposedly passive, grateful recipients. (Burchardt, 2004). Shakespeare and Watson (2002: 14) suggest that 'a social model view – in which the problems arose from social oppression – was and remains very liberating' and has spurred many on to social activism. The need for collective action to effect change at a societal level, and the central role for democratic organisations comprising of disabled people, are stressed. That people who live with impairments are the experts on their lives and fundamental to the co-production of knowledge and development of effective services is a central principle.

One important distinction made by authors in discussing the social model of disability is between impairment and disability. Impairment is a condition of the body or mind, such as lacking a limb, being partially sighted or experiencing psychosis. It is an attribute of an individual. Disability is the loss or limitation of opportunities to participate in the life of the community and society on an equal level with others that arises from the social, economic and physical environment in which people with impairments live (Burchardt, 2004). Finkelstein (1980: 47) explains that 'disability is the outcome of an oppressive relationship between people with impairments and the rest of society'.

Since the development of the social model, disability activists and academics have debated the relationship between impairments and disability, with questions asked about whether a focus on social barriers obscures the lived experiences of people with impairments. Shakespeare and Watson (2002: 11) argue that 'we are not just disabled people, we are also people with impairments, and to pretend otherwise is to ignore a major part of our biographies'. They argue for an approach that acknowledges disability is caused both by impairment and social exclusion, the latter amounting to social oppression, 'as people are disabled both by social barriers and by their bodies' (Shakespeare and Watson, 2002: 15).

Thomas (2004) suggests that the position that impairments and chronic illness do not cause any restrictions on a person's life is an impoverished version of the early UPIAS understanding of the social model disability. She argues that much of the original social-relational understanding of disability has been lost over time. A social-relational view means that it is entirely possible to acknowledge that impairments and chronic illness directly cause some restrictions of activity. But disability is a form of social oppression involving the social imposition of restrictions of activity on people with impairments and the socially engendered undermining of their psycho-emotional well-being (Thomas, 1999: 60).

Feminist and postmodernist theorists within disability studies have argued that the social model has not reconciled the dimensions of gender, race and sexuality within or alongside disability (Morris, 1991, Vernon, 1996). Central to their critique is the role of culture and cultural processes in shaping society and how differences such as gender, ethnicity, sexuality and type of impairment intersect to construct people's positions (Terzi, 2004). It is argued that to assume that disability is always the key aspect of someone's identity is to replicate the error made by the medical model perspective, which defines people on the basis of their impairment (Shakespeare and Watson, 2002).

Oliver (2013) reflecting on the debates, 30 years on, argues that he did not suggest that attention to individual experiences of impairment should be abandoned or claim that the social model was an all-encompassing framework within which everything that happens to disabled people could be understood or explained. However, he also argues that focusing on impairment and difference de-politicises the social model. Oliver (2013: 1026) suggests that, as he and others predicted, 'emphasising impairment and difference was a strategy that was impotent in protecting disabled people, our benefits and services, from the (post financial crash) economic firestorm', arguing it has caused deep divisions and left disabled people at the mercy of an ideologically driven government.

Over time, the concept of a social model has been extended to various areas, including learning disability (Barnes, 2012), mental health (Beresford, 2002), end-of-life care (Brown and Walter, 2013) and dementia (Thomas and Milligan, 2015). In their study of mental health service users' views about social approaches to madness and mental distress and their relationship with the social model of disability, Beresford et al (2010) found that most participants expressed reservations about whole-scale adherence to a social model, stressing the complexity of mental health problems. However, they suggested that their experiences of mental health issues fitted broadly within a social model approach, as mental health was impacted on by broader social and environmental factors. There was significant agreement that the existing medical model of mental illness is limited and can have negative effects. On the other hand, some potential problems with adopting a social model of disability approach were also identified, including not wanting mental health problems to be seen as an impairment and resistance to being stigmatised. Some participants argued that there was a real need for a related but different social model of madness and distress, in order to create solidarity among campaigning groups and to make clearer how individual distress might be associated with broader social relationships based on oppression and discrimination. Participants also highlighted that such a social model needed to take account of personal (for example, psychological) as well as social issues associated with mental ill-health (Beresford et al, 2010).

A paper on a social model approach to dementia (Mental Health Foundation, 2015) suggests that it provides an alternative framework to rethink and reimagine dementia as a rights, social justice and equality issue. The authors argue that 'pursuing a social model approach would bring a shift away from deficit-based thinking in terms of public discourse and policy for people with dementia, which frequently views them as somewhat less human and less deserving of respect' (Mental Health Foundation, 2015: 20). They too stress the need to take account not only of the external barriers, but also of the social and psychological obstacles that exclude or restrict full participation in society. Lived experience, as well as societal responses, also vary significantly depending on the severity, perceived 'stages', and the type of dementia.

As discussed in the Introduction, Pearce (2013) is unique in using the social model in child protection, where she applies it to considering issues of consent in relation to child sexual exploitation. She highlights the importance of recognising the factors impacting on the capacity for the young person to give/get consent, including social and environmental influences (being groomed, previous familial abuse, peer group pressure); structural influences (economic pressures, housing problems); professional influences (contact with school and teachers, and other agencies).

It becomes much more problematic, we recognise, when we attempt to use the model more broadly in relation to children of all ages with very different levels of vulnerability. As indicated above there have been controversies within the disability movement in relation to whether a focus on social barriers obscures the lived realities of pain and impairment. A complementary question for a social model of child protection arises: is there a danger when focusing on social contexts that the gaze becomes too broad and we deny or excuse the suffering of individual children? We recognise and own the uneasiness this can leave us with because it is in this space that truly reflective conversations can happen:

> Ours is a time of uneasiness and indifference – not yet formulated in such ways as to permit the work of reason and the play of sensibility. Instead of troubles – defined in terms of values and threats – there is often the misery of vague uneasiness; instead of explicit issues there is often the feeling that all is somehow not right. Neither the values threatened nor whatever threatened them has been stated; in short, they have not been carried to the point of decision. Much less have they been formulated as problems of social science. (Mills, 1959: 11)

It seems some things recur, particularly unease, and in our view, child protection practice needs to be reformulated as a matter for a social science of help. In seeking to reconnect biography, history and social circumstance, we have identified the following inter-related elements of what might be a better way to practise in child protection. We explore these in turn, building on and expanding the ideas advanced in the Introduction.

Understanding and tackling root causes

While we advance some key and often neglected themes here, we recognise that there is much more discussion to be had about root causes and, indeed, we hope this book promotes such discussion. By now it must be clear, however, that we consider the social and economic circumstances of children matter enormously. They are interwoven with what happens within and between people in intimate places. They require fuller consideration than they receive within our current paradigm.

There is a degree of consensus that material poverty and the related social problems harm children's development. *The State of Child Health Report 2017*, published by the Royal College of Paediatrics and Child Health (RCPCH, 2017) provided data on 25 measures of the health of children and found that across almost all the indicators in the report, children and young people from deprived backgrounds have worse health and well-being than those from high socio-economic groups, and in many cases the inequalities have widened over the past five years. What of the evidence on the relationship between poverty and the harms children experience? This is contested territory. For example, it is often noted by policy makers, practitioners and managers that not all those in poverty harm their children and indeed that those not in poverty do harm their children. Our research reveals that for social workers part of the resistance to examining the relationship between poverty and child abuse is a desire to avoid stigmatising families. It has become a conscious decision based on a commitment to avoiding oppressive practice (Morris et al, 2018a). The real risk here is that in seeking to avoid stigma the everyday reality of family life is ignored and hardships denied.

Academics are often shy of invoking a causation framework and engaging with discussions on causes. Lakoff (2014) offers some very helpful insights into why this might be so. He notes that every language in the world has in its grammar a way to express direct causation but no language has a way to express systemic causation. For him the difference between the two is as follows (pp 36–7). From infanthood on we experience direct causation: we push a toy and it topples over, we pick up a glass of water and take a drink, we use a knife to slice bread:

> Any application of force to something or someone that produces an immediate change to that thing or person is direct causation. When causation is direct, the word *cause* is unproblematic. We learn direct causation automatically as children because that's what we experience on a daily basis. Direct causation, and the control over our immediate environment that understanding it allows, is crucial in the life of every child. That's why it shows up in the grammar of every language.

By contrast, systemic causation cannot be experienced directly. It has to be learned and studied and repeated communication is necessary before it can be widely understood:

> No language in the world has a way in its grammar to express systemic causation. You drill a lot more oil, burn a lot more gas, put a lot more CO_2 in the air, the earth's atmosphere heats up, more moisture evaporates from the oceans yielding bigger storms in certain places and more droughts and fires in other places, and yes, more cold and snow in still other places: systemic causation. The world ecology is a system – like the world economy and the human brain.

Lakoff argues that systemic causation has a structure – four possible elements that can exist alone or in combination: a network of direct causes, feedback loops, multiple causes, probabilistic causation. Systemic causation is familiar. For example, smoking is a systemic cause of lung cancer. HIV is a systemic cause of AIDS. Driving while drunk is a systemic cause of car accidents. A systemic cause may be one of a number of multiple causes.

As Lakoff argues, semantics matter. Because the word cause is commonly taken to mean direct cause, climate scientists, for example, trying to be precise, have too often shied away from attributing causation of a particular hurricane or fire to global warming. Systemic causation has, therefore, mostly gone unframed and unnamed. However, according to Lakoff, across many complex issues (from climate to war to welfare), conservative moral frames tend to use the 'direct causation' metaphors (for example, 'Bush toppled Saddam and freed the Iraqis'). So much political debate appears to have followed this kind of direct-cause metaphorical mode, and for so long, that we usually do not even notice it operating.

This is helpful when thinking about how the relationship between poverty and child welfare is often framed. The direct causation metaphor has been used often within a frame that sees the individual's poverty as due to their failure to obtain work. It focuses on the agency of individuals. Multiple, complex causation is misleadingly reduced, via metaphor, to single, direct causation (for example, 'hard work leads to prosperity'). The mantra of 'hard-working families' is used to reinforce the message that poverty is caused by not finding work.

We recognise that a focus on systemic causation might be unhelpful as it could obviate individual agency. However, those advocating the value of an approach using framing argue that systemic framing does not imply a denial of individual control or agency (as factors). Instead, the analysis suggests in essence that the individual controls some factors, but not others (availability of income, costs of housing). So, it seems clear that we should use frames of 'systemic causation'. These are hard to do as newspaper headlines have, for decades, presented an extreme form of 'direct causation' promoting a simple link between idleness and poverty.

It is even harder to develop this notion of systemic causation in relation to poverty and child abuse and neglect. In part, this may be due to a historical absence of robust research (and this absence could be argued to be a result of anxieties about further stigmatisation). However, more recently we have seen the development of a body of studies exploring the relationship between poverty and child abuse and neglect, particularly in the US and now in the UK.

Bywaters et al's (2016) review of the evidence on the relationship between poverty, child abuse and neglect (CAN) concluded that there is a strong association between families' socio-economic circumstances and the chances that their children will experience CAN, and that there is a gradient in the relationship between family socio-economic circumstances across the whole of society, which mirrors the evidence about inequities in child health and education. The evidence suggests that the influence of poverty works directly and indirectly (through parental stress and neighbourhood conditions), and also in interaction with other factors, such as domestic abuse, mental health and substance abuse. While poverty is neither a necessary nor sufficient factor in the occurrence of CAN, it is one factor but perhaps the most pervasive according to this review of the evidence.

Multiple studies exploring the everyday lives of families in poverty provide important insights into the stresses and difficulties (see Featherstone et al, 2014). This work captures the tough choices families must make and the precarious nature of daily life.

The research on inequality obliges us to focus not just on poverty – although there is complete agreement on its crucial importance for everyday survival – but also on issues such as the relationships between different groups in society in terms of trust and distance and the differing types and rates of social problems faced by people. Wilkinson and Pickett (2009: 33) argued that more unequal societies have diminished social cohesion and augmented social problems. They suggested that 'individual psychology and societal inequality relate to each other like lock and key'. Similarly, Frost and Hoggett (2008) described how the experience of domination and exclusion produces social suffering, which has destructive consequences for the self and others. Friedli (2009: III) suggested that 'levels of mental distress among communities need to be understood less in terms of individual pathology and more as a response to relative deprivation and social injustice, which erode the emotional, spiritual and intellectual resources essential to psychological wellbeing'.

Friedli (2009) used the term psycho-social to highlight the psychological, emotional and cognitive impact of social factors, the effects of which need to be distinguished from material factors. She argued that 'individual psychological resources, for example, confidence, self-efficacy, optimism and connectedness are embedded within social structures: our position in relation to others at work, at home, and in public spaces'. It is therefore an ongoing challenge to separate out contextual effects that may be 'masquerading' as individual attributes or the effects of individual characteristics (Friedli, 2009: 9).

As we have indicated in the earlier discussion, this kind of thinking is largely unexplored in child protection. Eckenrode et al (2014) carried out a study in the US showing a link between inequality in different counties and levels of maltreatment. However, this is quantitative work and does not offer any findings in relation to how the link operates. More generally, the work on inequalities has not been drawn on systematically in terms of its implications for understanding the harms individual children and their families in particular places and spaces suffer. Thus there is a value in developing this work. Given, as we have highlighted, the evidence of high rates of parental mental health difficulties, substance misuse issues and domestic abuse (all prevalent in highly unequal societies) in families where child maltreatment occurs, a better understanding of the relationship between inequality and child abuse and how it is played out in particular life histories across time and space seem pressing issues.

Wilkinson and Pickett have not explored inequality through the lens of intersectionality. This is of concern and merits further attention. An intersectionality lens obliges attention to how inequality is played out in the lives and circumstances of men, women, black, white, those who have a disability and so on. Studies tend to focus on a single category of difference, for example ethnicity or gender, with less attention paid to intersectionality or how multiple categories interact in their effects. In part it may be the absence of data that makes such analysis possible, and it may also be in part due to the sheer complexity of trying to arrive at a holistic analysis.

The literature on child maltreatment and child protection does not, in the main, address the multiple interlocking identities at the micro level with inequality at the macro level of society. There are green shoots, with studies emerging that include elements of international comparisons and focus on communities and localities (Nadan et al, 2015). Researching material poverty and how this interacts with other forms of 'status inequality' (Fraser, 2008) is also uncommon. There are exceptions, for example Burman et al's (2004) study of domestic violence services to minoritised women. They highlight the 'over-emphasizing [of] the role of culture at the expense of analysing its intersections with gender inequalities and relations' (Burman et al, 2004: 352).

One result of this absence of complex analyses of intersectionality in CAN is the allure of accessible accounts of 'what works'. Thus, social workers wanting to develop effective responses to the harms children experience are left with a knowledge gap and slip readily into instrumental debates about the relative values of different programmes or techniques. The all-pervasive focus on harm and risk at the level of the individual child has meant that we lack critical empirically based knowledge about children's pathways and trajectories that can generate alternative approaches to supporting children and families.

Rethinking the role of the state

In the Introduction we noted the importance of a literature on social harms. Rather than attempting to calculate individual risk, social harm theorists identify collective responses to personal injuries. Indeed, a social harms lens reveals that the most pervasive and intractable social injuries derive from the pursuit of particular political and policy directions rather than intentional actions or personal deficits.

Pemberton (2016) examines comparative rates of homicide, suicide, obesity, road traffic injuries, poverty, financial insecurity, long working hours, youth unemployment, social isolation, and infant mortality across 31 countries. This analysis demonstrates how different policy regimes affect, for better or worse, these particular issues. Pemberton outlines how nation states can be categorised in relation to the harm reduction strategies they pursue. He then assesses the variance of statistical indicators of these harms across the different regimes. His analysis demonstrates that regimes that are characterised by highly individualised societies with weak collective responsibility for others, a minimal welfare safety net, and heavily privatised and means-tested social services, are associated with the highest levels of social harm. In contrast, social democratic regimes were found to be the least harmful.

Pemberton identified three aspects of social democracies that appear to reduce the incidence of social harm. First, social solidarity is evident, in the form of low levels of inequality and high levels of empathy towards others. Second, the dominant approaches separate the worth of human beings from their ability to accumulate wealth and thus provides generous universal welfare provision. Finally, the exploitation of workers is reduced through enforcing employment rights and supporting union membership.

These analyses highlight how differing forms of state decision making and organisation work to produce or reproduce social injuries and the need for social settlements that have a more collective focus (Gillies et al, 2017). As part of exploring how this project might be taken forward a variety of thinkers are reappraising the role of the state. This rethinking is very pertinent to protecting children, an aspect of the state's role that is both vital and extremely consequential for all concerned.

As we have highlighted in the Introduction we are advocates of robust state action to ensure rights and social protections. However, it is vital that we reimagine the state in the context of a number of very serious concerns about contemporary developments around centralisation, inequality and marketisation.

The UK remains one of the most centralised states within the Organisation for Economic Co-operation and Development (OECD) (MacKinnon, 2017). This has had a range of implications in relation to protecting children; while the delivery mechanisms are at the local level, policy and funding levels have been set centrally. Gillies et al (2017) discuss how policy in the area of early intervention, for example, appears to have become subject to capture by a range of interests that are not easy to trace, or indeed understand. Jones (2015) has illustrated some of these interests in relation to policy developments in children's services. A form of diffused network governance, described as a 'polycentric state' (Gillies et al, 2017), has been developed over time. This means a diverse policy landscape encompassing business, social enterprise, philanthropy and celebrities, voluntary organisations and others. In this context, it becomes increasing difficult to work out who is responsible for what (Gillies et al, 2017).

Regional inequality has also re-emerged as a major political issue in Britain in recent years as the effects of the post-2008 economic crisis have exposed stark disparities, particularly between London and the South East and former industrial areas and rural districts in the North and Midlands of England (MacKinnon, 2017). The study of geographies of inequality has developed a substantial body of work that sets out the unequal life chances of different communities and localities (Rae et al, 2016). Over decades loss has become a defining experience for many communities across the UK: loss of jobs, identities and local networks primarily as a result of economic restructuring. Such losses occurred in a context where public discourses became dominated by notions of individualised responsibility and risk and where the investment heralded by free marketeers largely failed to materialise (Davies, 2017).

As Davies (2016) so insightfully notes, the solution offered by New Labour governments post Thatcher was in Nancy Fraser's (2008) terms 'redistribution' but not 'recognition'. It created a 'shadow' welfare state, particularly through tax credits that subsidised poorly paid jobs. This was never publicly acknowledged, and co-existed with a political culture which condemned dependency:

This cultural contradiction wasn't sustainable and nor was the geographic one. Not only was the 'spatial fix' a relatively short-term one, seeing as it depended on rising tax receipts from the South East and a centre left government willing to spread money quite lavishly (albeit, discreetly), it also failed to deliver what many Brexit-voters perhaps crave the most: the dignity of being self-sufficient, not necessarily in a neoliberal sense, but certainly in a communal, familial and fraternal sense (Davies, 2016, no page no.)

Clarke and Newman (2014: 153) reflect on some of the features of a profound disenchantment with the state arising from marketisation and associated features:

Popular disenchantment with the state reflects the experiences of the kind of state we currently have to live with, at least in Britain – a state that has been commodified, marketised and managerialised, and sees to ignore the human relationships at stake in its encounters with citizens. But the 'rolling back' of the state also creates a strong sense of loss: the loss of state funded institutions (voluntary organisations, advice centres, arts and cultural provision), public services (the local library, hospital, youth centres), public welfare (elder care, childcare), and, not least, the capacity for public governance. In our current conditions of austerity and deepening inequality, many people are looking to the state to regulate financial interests, curb corruption and abuse, and prevent social harm. In such moments, we hear a different view of the state – it is seen as a bulwark against the market's destructive powers; as the guarantor of rights; as 'the equaliser'.

Clarke and Newman see the state as both an expression of something more than the sum of individual interests or choices, and also, paradoxically, as an instrument for the destruction and evacuation of public attachments and identifications. They propose an approach to it that enhances notions of the commons, reasserts collective interests and enables collective action. They propose a number of dimensions to this process. The first involves a stronger approach to public governance. Processes of marketisation and the dispersal of state power to a wide range of agencies – individual schools and hospitals, quangos, devolved bodies, voluntary agencies and corporations – have fundamentally shifted the relationship between public and private authority.

> We are left with thin forms of public authority and regulation that are getting progressively weaker with the recurrent attacks on 'red tape'. While there can be no going back to the monolithic state bureaucracies in which public governance was invested in the past, there is a need to explore how public authority and democratic legitimacy can be enhanced. (Clarke and Newman, 2014: 153)

The need to reimagine the state, advocated by Clarke and Newman (2014) as a dialogic entity, and to attend to, and nourish, dialogue in the context of public and political relationships that inform state action is vital, but complex and complicated. There are multiple publics, some of whom are much more needful of state action than others but also much more vulnerable to having their needs redefined in ways that may be very harmful to them. Moreover, the polycentric state makes it harder to track who is doing what to whom. In this context transparency, democratic scrutiny and debate become more necessary.

Thompson and Hoggett (2012) highlight additional issues of direct pertinence to our concerns in relation to enhancing dialogue about the ends and means of protecting children. They advocate for, and define, deliberative democracy as follows: 'A series of interlinked public spaces in which all citizens can participate in an ongoing free and fair debate leading to reasonable agreement – or even national consensus – on matters of public concern' (p 107). They note that it is vital that attention is paid to the probability that strong emotions will undermine principles of deliberation. They therefore argue that spaces should be structured not around the concept of 'rational argument' but as places where people can 'reveal their needs and express their emotions in a process of coming to what might be thought of as a "good enough" understanding of their fellows' (p 107). This is highly pertinent to discussions about protecting children.

Hoggett (2009) notes one of the functions of the state in democratic societies is to manage social divisions and the social suffering that arises from them and barriers emerge at a range of levels to opening up the kinds of discussions necessary:

> [S]uffering gives expression to the passive rather than active voice, to our needs as dependent rather than independent beings, to what is often chronic and enduring rather

than what is open to social engineering and quick fixes. So for both political and cultural reasons, Western-style democracies are partly in flight from suffering, and those who are the subjects of suffering become othered by an achievement-oriented, change-embracing modernity. (Hoggett, 2009: 164)

We explore this further in Chapter eight where we discuss how more helpful and hopeful stories can be framed to drive the change needed.

Just as we advocate continued discussions on root causes, continued discussions are needed about the role of the state on the part of all those involved in protecting children. In their exploration of particular policy initiatives, Barnes and Morris (2008) and Morris et al (2009) identified three overarching approaches to the value of the state guided by assumptions about the settlement between the state and families:

1. The state is a benign entity, and hand-holding children into mainstream services (for example mentoring schemes to get excluded children back into schools) is the most effective way of addressing and counteracting exclusionary processes and consequences and meeting children's needs. Shaping the child rather than the service is the focus.
2. The state is controlling and conforming, and separation and alternative provision (such as stand-alone education provision for travelling families) will keep children safe within their sub cultures and communities and avoid further demeaning and oppressive experiences that further dilute their heritage. The battle lies in seeking and securing the funding to sustain these services and avoiding appropriation.
3. The raison d'etre for services should be to bend and shape the assumptions underpinning services to arrive at provision that enhances participation, reduces inequalities and addresses children's immediate needs (a model based on 'and/both' and which included examples of services that delivered outreach services to refugee families while also working with schools to make their provision accessible and respectful). A multifaceted approach that demands high stakeholder collaboration and sustained funding to achieve embedded change.

This analysis provides useful food for thought when we turn to considering our project, and we see ourselves as located within the third approach. Our underpinning assumptions are that the state has a duty of care but that welfare responses must build on collaborative design rooted in everyday needs and experiences. It is not enough to change the child and the family (by case work or targeted interventions) or to separate the child/family (by removal or silo services). Our hope is to promote collaborative working between policy makers, managers, practitioners and families to develop robust knowledge about geographies, community capacity and vulnerability. Such a development would suggest a privileging of local knowledge and a move away from remote expertise or transient short-term services and policy making.

The contribution of the Capability Approach

The Capability Approach (CA) is a complex framework for the development of social justice that has been used in various different disciplines, such as economics, political philosophy and development studies, and for a variety of very divergent purposes, for example in measuring poverty or evaluating social policies. For the purposes of developing our ideas about a social model for child protection, we would argue there are some key elements of the CA that are particularly, but not exclusively, relevant, namely poverty and parenting; human rights and capabilities; and also the provision of a framework for evaluating policies and practices that focus not just on policy or organisational agendas, but on the lived experiences of children and families and their real opportunities to lead a life of human dignity and flourishing.

The CA is generally conceived as a flexible and multi-purpose framework rather than a precise theory. It calls for consideration of the role of social institutions to contribute to the development of individual freedoms or 'capabilities' to live the life the person values and has reason to value (Sen, 2009). The CA has informed ideas about human development, which is described in the first Human Development Report published in 1990 as follows:

> People are the real wealth of a nation. The basic objective of development is to create an enabling environment for people to live long, healthy and creative lives. This may appear to be a simple truth. But it is often forgotten in the immediate concern with the accumulation of commodities and financial wealth. (UNDP, 1990: 1)

The CA argues that people differ in their ability to convert means or resources into valuable opportunities (capabilities) or outcomes (functionings). Capabilities and functionings constitute people's well-being freedoms and well-being achievements respectively, namely the real possibilities and opportunities of leading a life which a person has reason to value, thereby generating more human development and flourishing in society. The differences in the capabilities to function can arise even with the same set of personal means for a variety of reasons or 'conversion' factors. Robeyns (2005) differentiates (at least) three sets of 'conversion factors':

- *'personal conversion factors'* such as physical condition, literacy, competences and so on that influence how a person is able convert the characteristics, commodities, infrastructures and arrangements into a functioning;
- *'socio-structural and cultural conversion factors'* such as social or religious norms, gender roles, power relations and hierarchies, discriminatory practices;
- *'institutional conversion factors'* such as welfare, health and educational provisions and community resources.

An understanding of the multi-dimensional influences on an individual's or families' capabilities and functioning is required. For example, a Bangladeshi Muslim woman from a traditional family background with limited English language skills and no recourse to public funds faces multiple barriers to her capability to leave her violent partner and safeguard her children. These could include institutionalised financial and practical barriers, fear of discrimination and social isolation within a racist and Islamophobic society, as well as gendered expectations of women's role within her culture and community.

The CA, therefore, like the social model of disability, recognises that people are not equally placed to realise their potential arising from structural inequalities and environmental and cultural factors, and tackling these is central to the CA's theory of social justice (Carpenter, 2009). The CA is predicated on a contextual notion of causality that is flexible enough to incorporate both individual and social causes into analysis (Smith and Seward, 2009). It highlights that whether individuals have certain capabilities depends not only on alleged individual features like skills and competences, but on the external conditions in which they find themselves, the norms, institutions and social structures that provide the setting of their actions and influence their ideas and actions. Not only is the acquisition of internal capabilities largely affected by external conditions, but also achieved internal capabilities may be restricted by a lack of opportunities for using these. Nussbaum (2011) refers to *combined capabilities*, which are freedoms or opportunities created by a combination of 'internal capabilities' and political, social and economic contexts that support these capabilities. By recognising that a person's capabilities are significantly shaped by their environmental and social circumstances, the capabilities approach encourages relational rather than individualistic thinking about people and their capabilities (Smith and Seward, 2009).

As discussed above in relation to social models, attention to individual differences is essential when considering lived experiences. The CA enables us to account for the diversity of human experiences, while also centring structural and policy arrangements within a social–relational framework. Many commentators have suggested that the CA does not sufficiently provide a critique of liberal individualism (Deneulin and Stewart, 2002). However Sen (2009: 245) challenges this when he argues that the CA is 'unequivocal in not assuming any kind of detached view of individuals from the society around them'. Robeyns (2003) suggests that the CA is ethically individualistic (each person of moral worth) rather than ontologically individualistic (the individual only for themself), as it acknowledges that capabilities and functionings are not independent of others and the experiences of individuals are embedded within wider social contexts.

Developing relationship(s)-based practice and co-production

In the Introduction and subsequent chapters we have highlighted the importance of understanding and rethinking relationships and developing practices that promote a broader and more creative project as part of the social model. This is not only necessary in respect of relationships between workers, children and their families in the context of feelings of fear, blame and distrust, but also based on the growing evidence of the importance of social relations to resilience, health and well-being and the damage caused by social isolation and loneliness.

In the 2000s, ideas about the importance of relationships to social work practice resurfaced through the development of relationship-based practice (RBP) as a challenge to the managerialism that emphasised reductionist understandings of human behaviour, narrowly conceived audit cultures and bureaucratic responses to complex problems (Ruch, 2005). Psychoanalytic concepts are central and complemented by ideas from attachment and systems theory (Ruch et al, 2010). While writers on contemporary RBP have emphasised the importance of an integrated understanding of individual and structural causes of social distress and practice within an anti-oppressive framework, theorising has primarily focused on intra-psychic and interpersonal dynamics (see, for example, Ruch et al, 2010 and Megele, 2015).

We absolutely see the importance of relationships. However, we would argue that *relationships*-based practice is a more porous approach that encourages an understanding of the surrounding contexts and recognises the multitude of relationships (helpful and unhelpful) in children's lives. As our earlier discussions suggest, we are proposing that it is critical to move beyond the individual relationship (which is often narrowly focused on particular household members and usually gendered). Instead we want to explore the opportunities to recognise children within their communities and to work productively and collaboratively within a number of networks. One example of an approach from the US that mobilises communities to protect children and support families is Strong Communities for Children. Strong Communities for Children is a comprehensive community-wide initiative for the promotion of family and community well-being and prevention of CAN (Kimbrough-Melton and Melton, 2015). The underlying premise is that to be effective, child protection must become a part of everyday life. The project emerged from diverse concerns and interests: the financial and human costs associated with an expert led system and a hypothesis that there was a link between child maltreatment, low social capital as well as material and increasing interest in community interventions to prevent maltreatment.

According to its founders, the ultimate goal is:

> to keep kids safe ... by strengthening participating communities so that every child and parent knows that if they have reason to celebrate, worry or grieve, someone will notice, and someone will care. Strong Communities involves the whole community through voluntary assistance by neighbours towards one another, especially for families of young children ... guided by the principle that people should not have to ask ... help should be built into community settings in a manner that is 'natural', responsive, and non-stigmatising. (Kimbrough-Melton and Melton, 2015: 67)

It is founded on the following assumptions and incorporates these in its design and implementation:

- Social and material supports are critical to children's safety.
- Community engagement can prevent child harm.
- This engagement needs to be universal, comprehensive and dependent on the engagement of volunteers and primary community institutions (for example, businesses, civic clubs and religious organisations).

By getting people noticing need and caring, it is argued that attentiveness to the experience of young children, and even more so their parents, is promoted. This in turn promotes neighbourliness as a community value and behavioural expectation and thus optimism.

No example is perfect, but alternative models do allow reflection on existing approaches. As we described in Chapter four, building dialogue and co-constructing services and practices offers a means of opening up new responses to supporting children and families. A conversation we have returned to repeatedly in developing this book has been the role of the social worker and the viability, indeed fairness, of asking the profession to drive the change we are identifying as needed. But there is an alternative perspective, one that suggest the changes we are proposing may lead to an easing of the load rather than to yet more difficult challenges to tackle. Increased family involvement has a track record of releasing social workers from overheated and, at times, unproductive narrow relationships. When Family Group Conferences (FGCs) were first introduced to the UK and families met in private to plan, social workers would reflect on how they felt the burden of responsibility had been lifted and shared, and how the family-led planning made it possible to practise collaboratively with the child's network (Marsh and Crow, 1996).

Embedding dialogic approaches to ethics and human rights in policy and practice

Supporting families and protecting children is complex work and there are rarely easy, straightforward answers. In the Introduction we discussed the concepts of 'moral distress' and 'ethical trespass' (Weinberg, 2009, 2016). Weinberg is a Canadian scholar from within a situated ethics approach who has carried out empirical research into social work decision making and ethics. She notes that in the field of nursing, a theoretical concept called 'moral distress' has developed, which identifies the psychological and emotional pain that arises when professionals feel blocked from doing what they consider is morally correct, due to institutional constraints. She argues that moral distress needs to be distinguished from the concept of ethical dilemma. Ethical dilemmas concern two or more courses of action that are in conflict (and will potentially have both positive and negative consequences), each of which can be defended as viable and appropriate. In contrast, moral distress arises if one action is preferred and seen as morally superior, but the person feels blocked from pursuing it by factors outside the self.

Weinberg argues the notion of ethical dilemma can eviscerate the political responsibility of social workers to be agents of change in unjust or inadequate situations. By contrast, moral distress involves perceptions of moral accountability and the degree to which a worker views themself as individually responsible or as restricted by circumstances.

She notes the contribution that evidence-based practice and proceduralism have made to changing social work from a 'practical-moral' activity to one that is 'rational-technical'. The fragmentation of the social work task where different parts of the 'problem' or different stages of a family's journey through care proceedings are dealt with in different parts of the system as explored in Chapter four offers many examples of this rational-technical approach. However, it is rarely understood as an ethical concern and, indeed, the notion of moral distress is not used in social work. This is puzzling for Weinberg, given the orientation social work has had to understanding the person in environment.

Weinberg points out some limitations with the concept of moral distress. She argues that it assumes the dichotomy of human agency and structure. In so doing, it can allow workers to sustain a stance of victimisation by the system. Practitioners, however, are not separate from their environment. Social institutions are the creation of human beings. Every time an individual enacts practice in a particular way, what constitutes social work is constructed at that moment.

A further limitation identified by Weinberg is that the notion of moral distress carries with it the assumption that there is an appropriate way of behaving. However, the field of child protection is filled with situations in which no correct response can be assured or entirely right. Sometimes, regardless of what stance is taken, both good and harm will follow. Workers contribute to dominant discourses of what is taken to be 'normal' (for example, normal standards of parenting). This power carries with it the potential to injure because some ways of being will be supported and others invalidated.

Weinberg notes this is the idea of ethical trespass; the harmful effects that inevitably follow not from our intentions but from our participation in social processes. For example, social workers, as people charged with responsibilities to determine norms, through the construction of those standards, judge some actions outside the boundaries of acceptable behaviour. Thus individuals who function beyond those boundaries can be disciplined for violations. Contributing to this problem is the reality that social workers usually have responsibilities to more than one service user at a time, such as in a family situation:

> Many philosophers speak about the third ... suggesting that if all of the world were just you and me, we could work things out; but in fact, there are always other people who are impacted by the decisions and agreements that we make between the two of us. So if I want to protect the singularity of a mother, that seems all well and good, but if she has a baby that is failing to thrive, and there is reason to suspect this problem is due to a lack of care being provided, my wish to honor the mother collides with the obligation to the third, namely, her baby. But if I focus on the baby and protecting his or her singularity, there are still the mother's needs and her humanity that I may violate. Either way, the social worker goes in her decision making, there is a third, and another third (such as the father or grandmother or other residents in a shelter for street-involved parents, and so forth). (Weinberg and Campbell, 2014: 41)

According to Weinberg, practitioners cannot ever fully know the complete extent of the consequences of their actions and thus are involved in ethical trespass. Consequently, workers must confront the harm inherent in their positions and be self-reflexive and humble in their practice.

These concepts were useful in the adoption enquiry (Featherstone et al, 2018), which confirmed the importance of a situated and dialogic approach to ethics that places dilemmas and decisions in a broader social, political and cultural context and sees responsibility in a wider, more relational sense, beyond the isolated individual decision maker (Banks, 2016). However, the enquiry also found social workers did not report many opportunities within their organisations to contest established practices or question whether a policy was right or wrong.

It is vital that organisational cultures are promoted that encourage ethical debate and discussion. It is recognised that individual practice is profoundly influenced by the organisational context, in relation to the practical realities such as time, size of caseload and access to resources, as well as the management culture of their organisations and the systems.

Just as families' lives need to be contextualised, so does attention need to be paid to the resources and cultures required in organisations to enable social workers and other professionals to practise in ways that promote human dignity and flourishing. This includes quality supervision and other safe spaces for critical reflection and dialogue, where values and assumptions can be explored and ideas such as ethical trespass and moral distress acknowledged and discussed.

Ideas of ethics and human rights are closely linked. So, the possibilities for ethical practice are compromised if there is not an active engagement with human rights. As mentioned in the Introduction, an inductive approach, which frames private troubles as public issues (what are the human rights issues at stake for this child and family?), requires the acceptance of a political dimension to problems (Ife, 2012). This discursive approach to human rights is consistent with a situated and contextualised view of ethics.

Concluding remarks

In this chapter we have sought to consider some of the theoretical and conceptual frameworks that can be drawn on in building an alternative model for supporting children and families. In the next chapter we turn to a more applied discussion, thinking about what the implications of our analyses are for practice and offering examples of alternative models.

SIX

A social model:
experiences in practice

Introduction

This chapter describes initiatives at a range of levels in order that we can promote conversations and open up possibilities. There is always a risk in presenting examples, but it is important when the critique of the existing child protection project has been so strongly argued, that we can recognise the many ways in which families and professionals are testing out new ways of working.

Looking forward, looking back: 'tidal hope'

When looking to develop practices within a social model, we need to look forward and consider alternative possibilities, but also not lose sight of what we know from previous studies about what children and families who are struggling find helpful. These stress the importance of practices of ordinary help that are rooted in working within specific communities and neighbourhoods. In *Re-imagining Child Protection* we noted the work of Jack and Gill (2010) and the histories of patch-based approaches and Sure Start (Featherstone et al, 2014). We have also seen the emergence of new models and frameworks for practice that are seeking to respond to contemporary harms, often digital. Locality and community take on a very different hue in these digital discussions, but cross-cutting themes of inequality and representation remain.

In exploring these examples we must recognise the realities for many deprived communities. Ann Power documents in her book *City Survivors* the strategies families must employ to survive in areas of urban decay (Power, 2007). More recently Darren McGarvey sets out the everyday realities for those enduring poverty (McGarvey, 2017). What is common across these apparently dissimilar accounts is the erosion of capacity within localities and communities to engage with well-intentioned services. In 2006 the national evaluation of the Children's Fund pointed to the same themes: deprived communities simply did not have the resources to work with services aiming to offer support

(Edwards et al, 2006). The evaluation team made the recommendation that, if support initiatives are to be successful, resources and time must be expanded on pre-building community capacity. Over a decade on, this message seems to hold even more true after a decade of austerity and the Great Recession. In a recent study of everyday life in a highly deprived community (Mason, forthcoming) a community leader described the community as living with 'tidal hope'. He was referring to the consequences for community engagement and trust of the ebb and flow of short-term-funded initiatives. This reinforces a message for any new approaches or models of the damage caused by the repeated experience of precariously funded social programmes.

We consider three themes in this chapter, loosely grouped as: disrupting the paradigm, disrupting the systems and disrupting practice. We offer some examples within each theme of initiatives that have sought to engage with the complex issues raised by our preceding analysis. We can only describe in many cases, we cannot comment on impact and outcomes beyond the information we hold, but the value of the examples lies in the conversations we hope they may provoke.

Disrupting the paradigm

That we need new conceptual and applied frameworks for supporting children and families is clear from the preceding chapters, but developing these when they rub so hard against the existing order is challenging. Krumer-Nevo provides an alternative framework that seeks to draw together emerging knowledge of social harms and case work responses of social workers to individual families with difficulties. It gives a central role to thinking about the social and economic determinants that must be addressed if children are to flourish and families are to safely care. The Poverty-Aware Paradigm (PAP) (Krumer-Nevo, 2016) can contribute to our understanding of the translation of critical social work ideas into practice, including within a social model for protecting children. We dwell in detail on this model because of the multiple opportunities it presents to bring together the analyses we have offered, and the potential it holds to build alternative practices and approaches.

The PAP requires attention to understandings of the nature of poverty (ontological notions), the ways this knowledge is acquired (epistemological notions) and ethics (axiological notions), which together shape the way in which practice is conducted, while social work practice itself influences and shapes these components as well (Krumer-Nevo, 2016). While not specifically aimed at child protection work, the ideas of PAP have much relevance to the development of a social model for protecting children. In particular, we highlight in this chapter the importance of attention to values and beliefs about the causes of inequality and how these fundamentally influence practice; the recognition of symbolic as well as redistributive injustice; and workers' use of power within relationships.

Three approaches to poverty are contrasted in Krumer-Nevo's (2016) work on the PAP. While the conservative approach places the responsibility for both poverty and poverty-related distress on people in poverty, the structural approach places it on societal institutions. The first approach views the solution for poverty in transforming the personal characteristics of people living in poverty through decontextualised, individualised means, an approach that we have argued is currently dominant in child protection practice. The second approach sees it as a matter of changes in policy, in the political arena and specifically through politics of redistribution. While supporting the underpinning principles of a structural approach, Krumer-Nevo (2016) argues that it fails to engage with the realities of everyday practice that connect the political and the personal, specifically in relation to the lives of people in poverty.

A third, the PAP approach, builds on and extends the structural analysis of poverty, viewing poverty not only as a lack of material and related social capital (for example, adequate housing, education and health), but also as a lack of symbolic capital. This is manifested in stigmatisation, discrimination, 'othering', denial of voice to and the knowledge of people living in poverty (Lister, 2004). The inclusion of relational/ symbolic aspects when thinking about the impacts of poverty and inequality shed light on the micro-level aggressions poor people experience every day, in which they feel the effects of stigmatisation, shame and powerlessness. This approach requires attention to the psycho-social impacts of poverty and inequality. Importantly it also requires workers to critically reflect on their role in perpetuating (and resisting) a hegemonic discourse that encourages us to see poor people as 'others' and the shaming practices that inevitably follow.

The PAP views poverty as a violation of human rights, and recognises the agency of families and their resistance to their poverty. Professional knowledge is viewed as the production of an ongoing dialogue and close relationship between social workers and the families with whom they work. These relationships are a significant feature of PAP practice. A qualitative study that explored the practice of a special poverty-aware social work programme from the perspective of women receiving services found that satisfaction was derived from relationships with workers that understood and intervened in their 'real-life' contexts, that is, the homes and communities in which they lived; attended to power relationships and challenged hierarchies; and focused on both material and emotional needs and their fulfilment (Saar-Heiman et al, 2017). The process enabled the women's material and emotional needs to be met: 'because alongside the practical implications of the focus on needs, being visible, having someone to stand by you, and close relationships are, of themselves, emotional needs' (Saar-Heiman et al, 2017: 1061).

While the PAP focuses on poverty, it is recognised that attention to inequality requires consideration of 'the intersection of poverty with other marginal positions – gender, ethnicity, race, sexuality and disability – in order to give us a fuller, and more accurate, picture of what poverty is for the various people who experience it and to avoid an essentialized and unified conception of them' (Krumer-Nevo, 2017: 818).

One strategy suggested by PAP is working in the real-life contexts of families' homes and neighbourhoods. Meeting service users on a regular basis at their neighbourhoods and homes is different from the narrowly defined 'home visit' often used for surveillance and monitoring. It is aimed at understanding the places and contexts of families' lives (Krumer-Nevo, 2017). For child protection social workers spending time with, and getting to know, families in their own places and spaces can help them understand and make visible what life is like for them, in relation to hardships, but also strengths and acts of resistance, especially where the primary aim is to help fulfil needs (rather than risks), including the child(ren)'s need for a safe and nurturing home (Saar-Heiman et al, 2017).

Linked to this, Krumer-Nevo (2017) suggests the importance of active mediation and advocacy, based on the recognition that the lack of symbolic capital among people in poverty makes it easier for others, including housing departments and benefits' agencies, to ignore their rights or to humiliate them on a personal level. Having a professional advocate and witness to injustices and 'micro-aggressions' can provide practical benefits and emotional support.

An example of an attempt to grow from within the community the services and practices needed to support children and families is the 'community mobilisers' (CM) scheme developed in the early 2000s. The following is a set of reflections on the programme by the lead manager at the time of development:

> In 2002 when staff were planning the Children's Fund Development Plan they saw direct work with high need

communities as a priority. This caused problems straight away as most of the other programmes in the region (South East) were focused on work with individuals. At first the programme was not accepted by commissioners or local agencies, there was considerable resistance to an approach that was not focused on individual change programmes (for example parenting classes, mentoring, anger management) and instead adopted a holistic approach to communities experiencing high need. The project was eventually passed in September 2003. This work continued until July 2012 (See https://communityactionmk.org/2015/07/31/the-end-of-community-mobilisers/).

They deployed 8 CMs in the highest need areas in Milton Keynes (this was mapped using deprivation indicators alongside data about children's service use). The brief was simple: to work with local people to strengthen or build from scratch preventative services for children in the age range 8–13 (driven by the Children's Fund remit). For example:

- One area had a failing breakfast club that had originally consisted of three local women and all the necessary equipment and finance to give breakfast to 60 children each weekday morning. Now it was down to one increasingly dispirited woman, insufficient funding and one faltering toaster. In this case the CM worked with the community to reenergise the breakfast club and get it working on a sustainable basis.
- In another area they had a full sized swimming pool attached to a local secondary school that was closed to the community during all school holidays – although open to groups from outside the area with their own swimming coaches. The CM worked with local people to develop a pool lifeguard qualification. This meant the pool stayed open during the holidays, was accessible to local children and now offered employment to local residents.

Outcomes

> an increase in preventative services for children in the eight
> areas (that expanded to 16) developed with, and by, the
> communities
> a year on year fall in the number of new children becoming
> looked after in the 8 areas although the level of social work
> referrals into the areas remained fairly constant.

An ethnographic study of the service undertaken by Drake and colleagues (Drake et al, 2013) points to the strong theoretical roots of the service in international community development work compared to the UK early intervention models focused on individual preventive programmes concerned with abuse and neglect. This is important because, while having a common concern (the well-being of children), starting from a very different place the resulting services and practices diverge from existing child protection casework. Drake et al suggest the key to the CM approach is as follows:

> Crucially, the aim of the CM is not to take the responsibility
> away from the community members they work with, but
> to stand beside them and support them as they negotiate
> difficult or unfamiliar systems or services until they feel
> confident enough to negotiate them on their own. The
> description as 'professional neighbours' signifies their
> role as being grounded in care and concern for a fellow
> citizen, a neighbour, a friend, with the added benefit of
> being a knowledgeable community worker who has a
> good awareness of local services and available community
> resources – and, most importantly, how to access them.
> (Drake et al, 2013: 317)

This approach is of particular interest because the original guidance for the Children's Fund (the funders of CM) uses predictive risk modelling. (A relatively crude model was adopted that identified certain behaviours or circumstances as cumulatively accruing risk and the higher the number the more likely the area/group would secure funding.) The Fund assumed by targeting certain children and groups with various forms of early intervention they would see a change in children's trajectories. The community mobiliser programme was at odds with this, rooted instead in building and strengthening community capacity and addressing first those issues that mattered for local families and communities. This CM programme assumed such an approach would naturally result in enhanced well-being for children, effectively a reverse model to the one adopted by most schemes focused on those 'at risk' at that time. By adopting a different theoretical framework, the services and practices developed were profoundly different from the mainstream. The programme shied away from parenting classes, individual risk assessments or interventions focused on changing specific behaviours. Instead the community mobilisers worked with what mattered, and this focus on 'mattering' helped build trusted relationships.

Our research indicates that there is a long way to travel in order for social workers to be able to stand alongside the communities they serve in the way the CM promoted, not because of individual social worker resistance but because of the consequences of risk-saturated approaches and systems. Many communities bear the scars of multiple levels of deprivation and current services often reinforce and compound such losses through high levels of investigations and removals. Relationships that are already fragile are ruptured, further increasing the possibilities for fragmentation and loneliness.

In exploring the potential for practice approaches that work with and in communities, we noted previously an ethnographic study by Holland et al (2011) that explored how children were safeguarded through informal networks and how decisions were made to make formal reports of concerns. During the fieldwork they became interested in an area of activity they called 'community parenting'. They defined this as the informal, everyday, shared culture of looking out for, or looking after, children within the immediate neighbourhood. As the researchers note, it is important to recognise the real social and economic problems on the estate, strongly exacerbated by high levels of poverty. However, many analyses can overlook the positive aspects of life in such communities. We would argue that contemporary individualist models of social work practice do not include a concern with harnessing such aspects to support families to flourish. Indeed, we have noted the limits in understanding the everyday routines and practices in communities as a result of the distancing of practitioners from the communities they engage with (Featherstone et al, 2014).

Changing the framing and telling a new story for protecting children is explored in Chapter eight, but it is difficult to see how such imaginative initiatives as the CM can be sustained without a new story. Within the current paradigm it is either tough for theoretical frameworks such as the PAP to get traction, or almost impossible for programmes such as the CM scheme to secure long-term funding.

And, as earlier discussions indicated, caution is needed when tidal hope becomes normalised in community experiences.

Disrupting systems

We have discussed at length the manner in which existing protection systems and processes can translate into daily practices that move the focus away from the core business of children and their families. Instead the focus becomes one of risk management and performance accountability. Morris et al (2018a) found that the preoccupation with risk management and thresholds resulted in a separation of family core business (warmth, food, shelter) from what child protection practitioners see as their core business (risk and family dynamics).

We have seen some changes in systems and processes that seek to enable practitioners to work with families differently. Strengths-based and systemic models of practice with individuals and families, including Signs of Safety (SoS), have been developed to address deficit-based, risk-averse contexts. The SoS model focuses on future safety, implying future parental competence, and including parents in decision-making processes (Turnell and Edwards, 1999). Keddell's (2014) evaluation of SoS suggested that the model holds much potential for humanising responses to risk that are productive in terms of personal change, client engagement and child safety, but that 'its focus on the micro context of client's lives only may omit significant structural causes of risks to children, or overstate social workers' power within organisational and wider political policy contexts' (p 70).

Similarly Roose et al's (2014) research into strengths-oriented approaches highlighted the importance of a sound conceptual and theoretical grounding of strengths-oriented approaches. They argue that addressing power issues is not solely a matter of building reciprocal and empowering relationships with families, but demands a broadening of the focus of strengths-oriented social work to incorporate a political level. RBP and other models of practice with individuals and families, including strengths-based approaches, can reinforce a process of individualisation and pathologisation if the contexts within which the families exist and workers practise are not explicitly recognised and addressed (Gray, 2009, Roose et al, 2014).

As this analysis sets out, changing the systems and processes of child protection are critical if the potency of any individual casework theories of practice are to be realised. But the codification of child protection systems in the UK is such that to step outside these systems requires central government approval. It is worth reflecting on this for a moment. It reveals the extent to which we have detached families and communities from child protection arrangements; to build a service that matches local need (but may not fit within the child protection systems) a central government minister must become involved. The minister may not have visited the locality, they may never have met anyone involved in using or supporting the system needing to change. In the abstract this truly is a strange set of affairs and says volumes about the rigidity and bureaucratic nature of our current responses and their (non-) capacity to be flexible and responsive.

Leeds is one UK city that sought central government approval for change. Specifically, it wanted to replace initial child protection conferences (ICPCs) with FGCs. Leeds had developed the most comprehensive FGC service in the UK (Mason et al, 2017). Familiarity with both restorative approaches and FGCs was high within the authority following an intensive period of city training and staff development. FGCs were used across the city to assist in planning for children with care and protection needs, and with families where there was domestic abuse. The FGC would usually occur after the initial child protection conference where there were significant concerns about a child's safety; where concerns were lower and an ICPC was not deemed necessary families could be 'diverted' into an FGC. This approach increased the use of FGCs, and therefore family involvement in planning, however the coupling of the two systems (one family led and one professional led) caused difficulties for families and practitioners (Morris et al, 2016, Mason et al, 2017).

At the heart of this tension was the collision of two governing sets of principles. In one (FGCs), children and families were assumed to have rights and expertise and to be the most appropriate first base for planning. In the other (the ICPCs) professional expertise led the system as the necessary way to ensure risks could be managed and safe plans determined. When FGCs followed an ICPC the clash became apparent in practice questions: was the family meeting simply agreeing the professionals' plan? Could the family overturn the ICPC plan? How could the ICPC be sure family resources and knowledge were utilised?

Permission was given to Leeds to step outside existing child protection guidance and to use FGCs earlier in the system. This development brought its own challenges, not least the mobilisation of the anxieties of social workers and frontline managers. As one manager commented, "we're calling it the ICPC FGC pathway to avoid words like diversion or replacing, as it makes people anxious!" The work has progressed, moving along very gently to ensure all stakeholders remain supportive. The barriers were around managing risk and how, in particular, frontline managers felt about the shift to family-led planning in the context of concerns about children's safety. In this particular example, the city's social work team managers made the decision about whether to use the pathway, usually in discussion with an FGC team manager. And, as could be expected, social work managers who were already comfortable with FGCs were more likely to use the new system. (This is an interesting development, raising questions about the interplay between culture and systems, something repeatedly apparent in FGC studies (Morris, 2013)).

For professionals enmeshed in a system that censures staff for anything other than compliance, changes like this are challenging. Social workers in response to FGC developments have expressed concerns about families safely managing risk, about their (social workers') capacity to influence plans and the ways in which information can be shared. However, despite these concerns and anxieties, over 20 families have used the alternative approach, with professionals growing in confidence about the shift and initial anxieties proving to be unfounded.

Such examples of responses to system disruption point to both the fierce hold contemporary child protection systems have on professional practice (and the emotions generated about their practice) and the stark realities of trying to insert alternative models into the existing systems. As we discuss in Chapters two and three, challenging embedded systems is difficult. It is possible to raise questions about the extent to which FGCs can be feasibly be used as a lever for change in these conditions, or, indeed, whether any specific decision-making model can drive wider systemic change. In these circumstances, FGCs are an almost perfect example of the realities of the tensions between 'doing the right thing or doing things right' (Munro, 2011). This reinforces our broader argument for a nuanced understanding of the barriers to progressive developments our existing child protection paradigm presents, and how opportunities for change can be missed.

Disrupting practice

Shame is a central feature of unequal societies with chronic levels of anxiety and depression evident. Goffman's (1963) analysis is of value in such a context. He described the social hurt of stigma; the experience of the individual who cannot produce the 'normal' social identity required, who is aware that they do not come up to standard and of a personal failure to pass. The opinion formed by those making judgements does not stop at presentation, but encompasses moral judgements and imputes certain characteristics; the discrediting of the person impacts on the whole identity. The stigmatised person shares the same belief system as the rest of the culture so the standards incorporated from the rest of society equip them to be aware of what others see as their failing, causing them to agree that they inevitably do fall short of what they really ought to be. Shame becomes a central possibility.

Attempts to work positively with families where there are care and protection concerns must currently sit within what are often experienced as deeply shameful encounters. This third 'disruptive' example begins to explore how family expertise can be harnessed to improve services and in so doing begin to overleap shame.

An independent research project was conducted in one London borough to ascertain the views of families receiving child protection services. The responses from many of the families were negative, and reflected many of the concerns of family members that are outlined in the studies we have discussed in Chapter four. Following the conclusion of that project, the Local Safeguarding Children Board (LSCB) commissioned a family-led enquiry into the child protection system by the existing Family Advisory Board (FAB), which is comprised of family members and staff, particularly FGC coordinators. (This enquiry is also being supported by one of the authors and at the time of writing this book is still underway.)

The project is based on a participatory approach to research and the co-construction of knowledge. It involves a number of stages. First, the core group of family members was extended to include new members from a local group that supported young parents who had lost their children to care and adoption. Two workshops were undertaken to (a) further develop the methodology and refine the research questions; and (b) complete training as peer researchers.

Following this, family members undertake interviews and focus group discussions with other families and social workers and managers, with the support of FGC coordinators. The aim of the project is to identify ways of making the child protection processes more effective and inclusive. Other family members will assist with the transcribing and analysis of the interviews. Once completed there will be a working seminar bringing together family members and social workers and practitioners to present findings and discuss new practices that will form recommendations to the LSCB.

Preliminary discussions with family members suggest the need for an advocacy service for families involved in the child protection system and there has been interest in developing a parent peer advocacy scheme. The proposal would be to train and support parents who have experience of the child protection system to provide advocacy for other parents through telephone calls, emails and direct contact, drawing on their own experiences of the child protection system. The advocate will help parents to understand and navigate the process and will aim to 'translate' some of the unfamiliar terms and concepts used by professionals. It will also break through the isolation that arises, in part driven by shame and stigma.

Both the family–led enquiry and the parent advocacy project draw on international initiatives in relation to family engagement in child welfare and protection services (Ivec, 2013, Tobis, 2013). Ivec (2013) conducted an international review of models for supporting parent engagement. She noted a number of peer partner programmes that aim to promote the parents' perspective in child welfare systems, develop working relationships between social workers and parents, engage parents in services quickly, build knowledge and respect between parents and workers and allow parents to become informed consumers of child welfare services.

In Australia concerned academics, professionals and community workers actively joined with parents affected by child removal to form the Family Inclusion Network (FIN). The fundamental principle of FIN is that parents and families have a central and imperative role to play in the child protection processes of assessment and decision making when children are at risk of being removed or have been removed. FIN branches operate differently in different parts of the country. For example FIN Townsville is an organisation of family members (parents, grandparents and significant others caught up in the child protection system) and supporting members (many of whom are social work practitioners or students) who take on the role of being *Resourceful Friends* (Holman, 1983), supporting family members in meetings with the Child Safety Department and in the Children's Court. Family members are centrally involved in the FIN Townsville committee, which is active in systems advocacy, making submissions for changes in child protection policy and practice and meeting with key ministers and bureaucrats (http://familyinclusionnetwork.com/ fin-branches/).

The INTEGRATE approach developed by MAC-UK (Durcan et al, 2017) seeks to provide holistic and responsive support to excluded young people, and involve young people themselves in being part of the solution. We would argue principles of the project outlined below have much merit when considering whole family services as part of a social model for protecting children as well:

- young people known to the group being employed in projects as peer supporters;
- an explicit focus on building trusted relationships between young people and the staff team, with time proactively given to just 'hanging out' together;
- a range of roles for the multidisciplinary staff team – from therapist, advocate, employment and benefits advisor to community development worker;
- a focus on what young people can do, rather than what they can't;
- an easily accessible staff team – with staff 'going to' young people, whether in the streets or safe community spaces, and flexible and responsive staff who aren't bound by formal appointment systems;
- a focus on creating wider social change such as transforming services, preventing other young people from offending and creating films or music to express experiences to the wider community (Durcan et al, 2017: 1–2).

Peer support in child protection has limited traction in current practice. As our earlier discussions suggest, it is not simply a matter of bringing together families who are using child protection services. A cultural shift is required in order for families to be seen as having expertise to offer, and an investment of resources that avoid families being asked to offer support in a way that they cannot sustain, or are not ready to provide. Not all families can offer peer support safely or appropriately, but for others a reciprocal relationship may be an obvious next move. What is critical here is opening up the possibility of reciprocity and, with it, opportunities for maturing relationships.

Practising differently: Zara, Carla and Jamila's story

Individual social workers and managers also have power and agency to do (at least some) things differently to protect children and promote their and their family's welfare. Using a composite case study from one of the author's practice experiences, we explore how practice with individual families within a social model might look.

Zara is a 19-year-old Black British young woman of Caribbean origin. She was sexually abused by a family friend when she was young. She eventually told her mother, who believed and supported her, but Zara suffered from depression and at times her relationship with her mother was fraught. She left school and home at 16. At 17 she had a relationship with Carl, who is also Black British of Caribbean origin. Their child, Jamila, was born when Zara was 18. Zara and Jamila were living in bedsit accommodation, which in warmer weather was infested with cockroaches and in winter too cold. Her relationship with Carl was on and off. He would at times stay with Zara and the baby, but when there were problems he would move out and stay with friends. One time neighbours called the police because of an argument between them. Carl worked as a cleaner on a zero-hours contract, and often did not get work. Zara was in receipt of benefits. After an argument with Carl one day she took an overdose and was hospitalised. At the time of the overdose, Jamila was with Zara's mother. The local authority became involved and it was agreed that Jamila would remain with Zara's mother. However, when Zara was released from hospital she wanted Jamila returned to her care. The local authority then initiated care proceedings. The viability assessment of Zara's mother as a long-term carer for Jamila was negative and the local authority were not recommending the return of Jamila to either parent. Zara was assessed but her mental health and the conflictual relationship with Carl were considered too risky to return the baby to her care. During the proceedings she was offered no support from 'the child's social worker'. Carl asked to be assessed as a carer for Jamila, but was rejected after a brief assessment identified his previous convictions for cannabis possession, and the lack of stability in his life. The care plan presented in the court proceedings was for adoption.

Zara's ability to care safely for Jamila was compromised by her depression and suicide attempt, but limited attention seemed to have been paid to what may have been the underlying causes and how these could be addressed to enhance her capabilities to parent Jamila. The focus was on the assessment of risk rather than the provision of support. The history of abuse is vitally important to understand and explore in terms of her psychological functioning, and effective therapy could be of benefit. External factors, such as the conditions of her home and living on a low income, also made life much more of a challenge. Both she and Carl are young parents whose relationship was, at times, conflictual, although there was no violence. Her depression is likely to have placed a strain on their relationship, as well as his social circumstances (for example, a precarious income and homelessness). Her lack of confidence and feelings of difference due to abuse, poverty and being a young parent may have made it harder for her to access community support services, services which are in short supply, moreover, due to cuts. Her mother is supportive, but as a single working parent with three other children, she has limited time (all factors which contributed to Zara's mother being ruled out as a permanent carer by the local authority).

Practice within a social model would have involved working alongside both Zara and Carl, asking them what their hopes and aspirations were for their child and themselves, and what they felt limited their capabilities to care safely for Jamila. While adequate housing may not be easily resolved, at least this, as a stressor, needed to be recognised and actively addressed. A key strategy in the PAP is active mediation and advocacy to address the lack of symbolic capital so often experienced by people in poverty. Also rather than simply referring Zara to a children's centre, and then having her not attend due to feelings of stigmatisation, understanding her reluctance and working with what she felt would help increase her support is required.

Similarly, working with Carl to help him be involved in Jamila's care requires engagement with him about what services are available that he feels comfortable with and respected by. This may include engagement with specific services for young men which could also address his individual hopes for better training or employment. While the impact of Zara's mental health on Jamila cannot be ignored, proactive support from adult mental health services needed to be mobilised and, importantly, protective factors within both parents' family networks, with Zara's mother being key. Consideration needs to be given to their previously fraught relationship, but this also needs to contextualised in relation to her history of abuse and adolescent development.

Throughout, workers need to reflect on how the parents' identities as young black working class people have framed their lives and, importantly, affect the values and assumptions of professionals who work with them. Questions to be asked involve thinking about how 'othering' processes are further exacerbated through the prism of risk. For example, was Carl seen as more dangerous because of his race, gender and class? Similarly, how may assumptions about Zara's mental health have been influenced by her race and gender? To what extent was supporting Zara and Carl considered too risky in the current climate, and adoption seen as an 'easier' and 'safer' option? What does 'being the child's social worker' actually mean in practice, when Jamila's life is so embedded in family relationships. A dialogic engagement with the ethical and human rights issues so clearly inherent in this case example is essential.

The practice of the local authority in the case study described above is not unusual in the authors' experiences of practice and research, as discussed in Chapter four. Crucial issues for workers seeking to work in ways consistent with promoting social justice and human rights include problematising dominant discourses, recognising the complex psychological and social factors impacting on children and families' well-being, critically reflecting on their own and others' values and assumptions and, importantly, attending to relationships that enhance not diminish parents' capabilities.

Concluding thoughts

Within a social model for protecting children, a multi-dimensional and contextualised understanding of social problems is required, as are services and professional practice which address the lack of material, social and symbolic capital that cause harm to children and their families. In Chapter five we discussed social determinants of harm to children and families, the various material and emotional impacts on well-being, and their interrelatedness. We argued that an understanding of the multi-dimensional influences, individual, family, community and wider society, on an individual's or families' functioning is required, as are services that aim for transformative change at different levels.

For individual social workers working with individual families, as a start this means assessments, reports and plans recognise and highlight the structural underpinnings of families' hardships, making them visible to professionals and to the families who are the subject of the assessment/report (Weiss-Gal and Savaya, 2012). There can be a recognition that solutions to problems are not only about individual change, but also (sometimes primarily) reflect the impact of social and economic environments on individuals and families. Social workers can be mindful of the influence of dominant, contradictory discourses that reinforce individualised notions of risk, and 'us' and 'them' 'othering' processes on their and their colleagues' practice in highly risk-averse contexts. All these developments are difficult in risk-focused, indeed risk-saturated, case work approaches. The recent turn towards strengths-based case work may open up possibilities.

This, we argue, is an important focus for change. A small-scale evaluation by one of the authors of the work of a financial support worker project (FSWP) in a charity working with families where a child has a serious or life-limiting illness found that the worker made a significant positive difference to the lives of the children and their families, both materially and emotionally. The benefits of the service came from both the outcomes (for example, Motability scheme cars, help completing forms and securing entitlement to benefits) and the process of the work (for example, a relationship with the worker based on listening to, and supporting, parents and supporting them to achieve what they value for themselves and their children). These services were particularly important for families marginalised by factors such as race, class and language. The two researchers, both social workers, reflected (with some sadness) on how these were core social work tasks that had never been experienced by the families in their multiple interactions with the local authority. The responsiveness to practical and emotional needs, as well as advocacy, were key positive findings in Saar-Heiman et al's (2017) study as well, and, we would argue, are important components in relationship building within a social model for protecting children.

Recognition and respect are also crucial considerations when working with children and young people. Firmin et al (2016) stress the importance of choice, agency and recognising young people as key partners in (contextual) safeguarding themselves. While this does not mean that they hold responsibility for keeping themselves safe or necessarily 'know best', it means acknowledging that 'the efficacy of professional interventions is determined by young people's willingness to engage, and that those services which keep young people informed and involved in decision-making processes are most likely to be valued by young people' (Firmin et al, 2016: 2332).

Beyond the relationship with individual workers, attention needs to be paid to how children and their families' relationships with others can enhance their recognition, respect and resilience. This involves actively considering individuals as members of wider family and friendship networks and communities, and working with people already involved in families' lives whom they trust to develop protective and capability-enhancing supports (for example, proactive use of FGCs). It involves, crucially, addressing the social and economic barriers that could inhibit positive support. Morris (2013) highlighted the limits created when family is defined in practice as household. But working beyond immediate carers, even when practice methodologies are adopted that expressly promote this, is challenging. As Laird et al (2017b) found, without resourcing and cultural changes the default focus for practice engagement remains the household, and within this, mothers.

Other agencies and professionals have important roles to play as well, and alliances are important. The Academic Resilience Framework for schools provides valuable ways for the whole school community to help disadvantaged students achieve good educational outcomes despite adversity (www.boingboing.org.uk/defining-academic-resilience/). It involves teachers playing their part in recognising and addressing the 'basics' of adequate housing and income, as well as promoting positive mental health and prosocial relationships. Work by Hart (2016) using the Capability Approach to explore school meals also points to the value of broader understandings of children's circumstances being developed and supported in schools.

This chapter has highlighted the challenges facing those seeking to deliver change, but also what innovation can reveal about the existing paradigms and practices. In the following chapters we consider the critical need to develop a new story that can support alternative approaches. As this chapter has demonstrated, there are real limits to the change that can be driven by inserting new practices or models into the existing systems.

SEVEN

Domestic abuse: a case study

It is not actually possible to say anything. I occasionally notice. Words are general categories that lump together things that are dissimilar in ways that matter ... To use language is to enter into the territory of categories, which are as necessary as they are dangerous. Categories leak. (Solnit, 2017: 137)

Introduction

We are very mindful that domestic abuse illustrates the perils and possibilities of the approach we are promoting in this book. For example, there are clear dangers in an overly social approach to men and their use of violence that situates each and every one as an instance of the general and a reductive cipher. This can be evident in the approaches taken by 'perpetrators' programmes that eschew any engagement with biography, culture and context in favour of universalist understandings. However, there are comparable dangers in promoting approaches that cannot see the contexts in which gendered inequalities intersect with other inequalities such as those of class and 'race' and are played out in identities and practices where shame and humiliation are ongoing possibilities.

In *Re-imagining Child Protection* we made a plea for humane practices with men and women and for seeking to understand from them why so often their lives were marred by abuse and violence. We asked that practitioners talk to individual men and women about their hopes and dreams, their expectations for, and from, each other. Crucially, we suggested there was a need to integrate gendered constructions of masculinities and femininities with biographical and interactional patterns in order to more fully understand and challenge abusive practices and to eschew a hegemonic focus on risk and rupture.

In this book we recognise that although some very welcome practice developments have emerged in recent years, practice stories of risk and rupture remain all too common and there continues to be inadequate attention paid to exploring with men and women what lies behind their experiences of harm and pain. We locate our project within a clearer understanding than is to be found in *Re-imagining Child Protection* of intersectional analyses and their contribution to engaging with the causes of, and consequences of, abusive behaviours.

Risk and rupture: who gets hurt?

Kim has one child who has been adopted with whom she has letterbox contact and another child who lives with her. Her relationship with the father of the adopted child was characterised by extreme violence from him and she struggled to separate because of his ongoing harassment. Her father had also been violent to her mother throughout her childhood. Her understanding is that her child was removed because of her childhood and adult experiences of domestic abuse. She has re-partnered and she and her current partner have a child who now lives with them both after a lengthy assessment.

Kim's ongoing feelings of grief and loss about her child who has been adopted co-exist with a profound sense of injustice. She feels she has been punished for having a violent father and partner.

Her child is nearing school age and, as she is on benefits, she knows she will need to seek work or be sanctioned and have even less money than she has currently. Money is a constant worry now and she fears for the future where her only job prospects would appear to be in the 'gig' economy, characterised by very low wages, precarious working conditions and high levels of insecurity. She also worries that children's services might become involved again if she is considered to be neglecting her child because she cannot afford to access childcare when working antisocial hours. Her partner is also exposed to the same precarious job market with its unpredictable working hours.

Stories such as these are sadly commonplace and are key to the impulses to rethink and reimagine policy and practice in domestic abuse that are now apparent in many countries and across the UK. Before we discuss the possibilities some of these hold out, it is vital though to take a step back and interrogate some of the problematic assumptions that have impeded rigorous understandings of the causes and consequences of differing levels of vulnerability to violence and thus fuelled approaches that are insufficiently attentive to the differing circumstances and needs of women, men, children and young people.

Rethinking who and why in domestic abuse

> Part of the long-term view involves interventions to change perceptions and behaviour. This has to be based on an understanding of the factors that are driving prevalence and that these may vary from one community to the other. Domestic abuse is not limited to any ethnicity, sexual orientation or segment of society. It occurs across a range of demographic divides, although it occurs more often against women than against men. (JTAI, 2017: 13)

This account by a range of inspection agencies of their review of multi-agency arrangements in relation to domestic abuse and the protection of children reflects a common but actually a quite puzzling message: we need to understand the factors that drive prevalence but actually it is widespread and everywhere!

However, a range of scholars and activists have been rethinking for some time now the traditional feminist message that domestic abuse is widespread, victimises women, and occurs across *all* classes and cultures is (Nixon and Humphreys, 2010, Sokoloff and Dupont, 2005). In 2005 Sokoloff and Dupont (p 40) argued that both an intersectionalities perspective and a social structural perspective were needed to provide women from diverse backgrounds with the kinds of personal and social change required for safety and growth at the individual and communal levels. They argued that a 'traditional' feminist approach asserting the equal vulnerability of all women of all classes, ethnicities and cultures to violence was highly problematic and obscured complexity and the structural causes of violence.

Nixon and Humphreys (2010) have argued for the importance of attending to an evidence base that is constantly changing and being updated and also the importance of engagement with a rich body of work on intersectionality. Since then the evidence has indeed made clear that while it might be correct to say that domestic abuse occurs across all classes and cultures it is not correct to say there is equal vulnerability across all classes and cultures. A review for the Joseph Rowntree Foundation by Fahmy et al (2015) concludes that there is a host of evidence showing vulnerability to domestic abuse to be associated with low income, economic strain and benefit receipt. The mechanisms linking these are not well understood but the most common relate to the effects of financial strain on relationship stress and quality and issues arising from men's inability to fulfil the male breadwinner role. This evidence is not well known however:

> It was clear from our inspections that, in any given area, there were groups within the overall community where it was more difficult to prevent domestic abuse and where it was harder to protect victims and children. However, we found some examples of tenacious culturally sensitive work by partner agencies working together to challenge cultural norms or reach seldom-heard groups. (JTAI, 2017: 13)

This statement from the inspection agencies is followed immediately by reference to the work being done in Bradford a city in the North of England with a large Pakistani population. It is unclear what exactly is being said here. Is there more domestic abuse in Pakistani communities and if so this seems to moderate the rather sweeping claims made above about prevalence. It may also refer to the perceived difficulties in such a community in relation to speaking out. Either way while an academic treatise on domestic abuse might not be expected from such a document, it is unhelpfully ambiguous in its phrasing and out-of-date in terms of the evidence base. As Nixon and Humphreys (2010) suggest, the increased vulnerability to domestic abuse of minority ethnic women that is found in the research evidence from a range of countries is likely related to poverty and income, noting the evidence that minority ethnic families are likely to be poorer than white families.

The growing body of evidence also suggests that domestic abuse is not just experienced by women or, indeed perpetrated by men, although the most serious levels of abuse still continue to be experienced by women. Interestingly moreover, while the relationship with deprivation holds for women, it does not for abuse against men (Fahmy et al, 2015).

These analyses on the differing vulnerabilities of women to domestic abuse by implication raise issues about the differences between men and the factors in men's abuse. The relationship between poverty, masculinity and domestic abuse is underexplored. However, the recognition that poverty is a factor in domestic abuse and, as suggested above, is linked to men's perceptions of the breadwinner role suggests how vital it is to understand and engage with social constructions of masculinity.

Overall, given the extensive evidence that has emerged of the focus by child welfare and protection systems on deprived populations, the levels of domestic abuse that are commonly to be found in families subject to child protection processes are, therefore, to be expected and add fuel to our concerns about the invisibility of poverty in contemporary child protection policies and practices. Moreover, the Fahmy et al (2015) review, among other research, found that a range of system interventions can either trap women in abusive relationships or be a driver of their vulnerability to poverty post separation. This reinforces the need to critically interrogate the implications of system interactions including child protection systems. This is an international phenomenon as Goel and Goodmark (2015) noted in their work on comparative perspectives: 'gender-based violence exists on both the micro and macro levels; women disproportionately face violence at the hands of intimate partners *and* at the hands of the state, and those experiences of violence intersect to reinforce women's oppression' (p viii, emphasis in original).

Between domestic abuse and child protection

In England, the recognition that domestic abuse is a child protection issue, the legislative manifestation being the Adoption and Children Act 2002, has had mixed but often problematic impacts as we saw illustrated in Kim's story. While drawing attention to the harms that children can suffer as a result of the abuse between adults and, indeed, the coincidence often of abuse to women and abuse to children, the implications for mothers especially can be problematic. They can be judged as failing to protect and become invisible in terms of their own needs as women. There can be unrealistic pressures placed on them to keep children away from violent men (men they are themselves afraid of). 75% of child protection plans now are made in relation to emotional abuse or neglect with domestic abuse strongly implicated in both, and research suggests mothers can experience child protection services as blaming and punitive in such contexts (Featherstone et al, 2016).

A development in recent decades has been a concern over how women with children have had to manage different systems and services. Contact arrangements between children and the violent male partner provide a flash point for these concerns. The public law and private family law courts can place women in very complex and difficult positions where contact is used to continue abuse, but also can stop women building new abuse-free lives. Moreover, women can find themselves struggling to meet the demands placed on them in private law proceedings to allow contact at the same time as demands from child protection services that they have no contact with abusers – this can place them in impossible positions.

Though it is an extreme example in terms of its outcome for the victim, we can learn some things about the unintended consequences of the current service configurations and their practice orthodoxies by examining the findings of the domestic homicide review into the killing of Natasha Trevis in Birmingham in 2012, at the hands of her partner Junior Saleem Oakes, who had a history of mental health problems and drug use (http://birminghamcsp.org.uk/admin/resources/bdhr-2012-13-04-final-published-1.pdf).

At the time of her murder, Natasha was 22 years old with three young children under five years, subject of child protection plans under the category of emotional abuse due to their exposure to domestic abuse. Natasha had fled and been staying with her mother, but due to overcrowding she was in temporary accommodation at the time of her death. At the time of the killing, she had recently had a termination of another pregnancy. Professionals knew of this, and of her wish to keep this from Oakes. However, he found out and Natasha was fatally stabbed 29 times in a brutal attack. Oakes was charged shortly after the event and convicted in January 2013. He had a long history of violence, particularly to women. He had a troubled past of his own and subsequently killed himself in prison. Reading the review of this distressing case, we are struck by the typicality of the structure of agencies' responses. The case was marked by multiple transfers between teams and the familiar litany of missed opportunities:

> 86. The referral from the Police to the EDT Social Care team had been passed on to the Children's Social Care Referral and Advice Team. Internal agency records checks were made but checks with Health Visiting or the GPs involved with the children were not undertaken. The referral was passed on to the Duty and Assessment Team for the area, in which the victim lived, for a follow up initial assessment to assess the needs of the children. There was a delay in allocating this assessment and the victim was not seen by the social worker until the next month. The delay appeared from the records to have been related to difficulties initially in staffing levels and then in making contact with the victim.

The interventions, too, bear the hallmarks of the contemporary mindset, paragraph 118 notes the following actions, subsequent to the initial child protection conference:

> 118. Both parents were advised to attend a range of courses in different agencies that had not been represented at the Initial child protection conference or the following meeting: for example, the perpetrator was required to attend an anger

management course; the victim was required to attend a domestic violence for victims' course and both of them were advised to attend a 'promoting happier parenting' course. The availability or suitability of any such courses had not been assessed. It was recorded that the victim and the perpetrator had maintained to the Initial child protection conference that they were separated.

This 'programme' orientation is very emblematic of what is typically on offer and funded, although in the context of austerity increasingly unavailable. However, it is also indicated that practice was held in place by a moral story about the mother's responsibility to protect the children. The review notes:

> The assessment work carried out by the social worker supervised by the team manager from February 2012 to July 2012 demonstrated a lack of understanding of the dynamics of domestic violence and abuse. In particular, the social worker interpreted the behaviour of the victim as uncooperative and reluctant because she presented as vague and ambivalent about her relationship with the perpetrator. Information was provided by the victim and her mother on more than one occasion that the perpetrator was in control of what the victim said to the professionals even when he was not present himself. It was said that he threatened the victim with removing the children and reporting her as a bad mother and threatened her that the agencies would remove the children, if she said anything. As a consequence when the social worker on the first visit at the end of February 2012 recorded that it had been explained to the victim 'that child protection action might have to be taken, if she did not protect the children' the social worker was confirming to the victim what the perpetrator had said. Although social workers should be clear with families what their role and authority consists of, the approach was not sensitive to the victim's situation and served to reinforce the oppression by the perpetrator. (pp 43–4)

Thus, practice in child protection is often puzzling and paradoxical. For example, women who are experiencing domestic abuse are treated as individualised risks to their children with a focus on solutions such as leaving the men and/or ensuring the children have no contact. As individuals, they shoulder the risks of protection and the burdens of recovery – they alone are responsible, with little attention paid to the practical and psychological challenges of mothering alone. The men who abuse them often also receive a highly individualised response that instructs them to leave this particular family and have no contact. This, of course, means that they are often moving from one family to another causing untold damage and trauma. However, if they do access a perpetrators' programme and this is by no means at all certain, given resource issues, they may receive an overly reductive social approach which treats them as instances of the general, a categorical model where their individual life-stories are rendered irrelevant in a narrative of men's desire to have power and control. For example, Domestic Violence Perpetrator Programmes (DVPPs) were developed originally in the US in the 1980s and were concerned to move away from therapeutic, particularly psychodynamic approaches. In their initial development they were envisaged as one part of a wider Co-ordinated Community Response to domestic abuse. This aspect has not always been developed fully as they have been rolled out worldwide although many are embedded in local arrangements in the UK (Kelly and Westmarland, 2015).

They are group work programmes based on cognitive behavioural approaches and underpinned by a feminist understanding of the role played by power and control issues in men's motivation to abuse and the group work for men is accompanied by support services for women. Men's abuse is considered a rational strategy to keep power and control in relationships and there does not appear to be a coordinated focus on the complexities attendant on their use of violence. For example, how do men internalise the shame of being unable to access the male breadwinner role? How do they cope with not being able to provide for their families? Are they able ever to articulate this or does it remain hidden and probably more damaging and dangerous therefore? How do they make sense of their own lives in the context of socially validated constructions of masculinity that stress men should be able to manage their emotions, be self-supporting, rational and independent? Indeed, we would suggest highly rational treatment approaches can run the risk of reinforcing the very behaviours that are key to the violence in the first place.

While children are allegedly central to protective practices, Callaghan et al (2016) note how those experiencing domestic abuse are typically described in academic and professional literature as passive and damaged. The clinical language of damage and trauma obscures the ways in which children make sense of and resist the violence. 'Damaged' suggests being broken and increasingly this is articulated in biological terms. Using data from interviews with, and drawings by, children, the authors show the objective pain of abuse, but also how:

> [a] failure to 'hear' children's corporeal resistance entrenches the idea of passive and docile victims .... Rather than being entirely 'unmade' by the violence, rendered silent and as object, their corporeal resistance in body and space speaks volumes, articulating, and therefore establishing, the very subjectivity that language of violence seeks to undermine and control. (p 416)

Seeds of change?

Overall, there has been a fragmented and siloed approach to families in a context where there is a great deal of fear and distrust of child protection services. There have been few services to support families who wish to stay together with a consequent focus on separation and rupture. All these issues are now subject to scrutiny and critique and the consequent development of new practice initiatives. For example, a 'whole family' intervention in Doncaster has been designed and rolled out to meet many of the concerns above (see Stanley and Humphreys, 2017).

As noted previously, there have been also been innovations in practice in local authorities such as Leeds, with the use of family group conferencing in the context of a wider engagement with restorative approaches (Sen et al, 2018). These are related to developments in restorative justice. As Ptacek (2010) notes, restorative justice is most commonly applied to youth crime and is concerned to develop mediation practices that seek to decrease the role of the state in responding to crime and increase the involvement of personal, familial and community networks in repairing the harm caused by crime. In many countries it is prohibited from being used for crimes against women. Nevertheless, it is increasingly being used to address intimate violence, rape and child sexual abuse. This increasing use has been controversial with many feminist anti-violence activists (Ptacek, 2010).

However, feminists such as Joan Pennell (see, for example, Pennell and Kim, 2010), in the US, work within restorative justice, noting that state responses to violence and child abuse have led to mother blaming and child removal and there has been a reliance on legal interventions that often backfires on poor women and women of colour. She has been concerned with whether advocates for women and children can collaborate with state institutions without becoming co-opted to goals that run counter to their beliefs and has been developing what Ptacek (2010) calls hybrid models.

We consider developments such as these are important to explore for a number of reasons. They emerge from a strong understanding of the ways the state and state agencies can further reinforce the oppression of already multiply disadvantaged communities and they thus seek to increase the involvement of family and community networks in repairing the harms caused. They are explicitly designed to restore relationships and counteract the fracturing that can occur through interactions with justice or child protective services. Because of their origins they are highly attuned to the importance of culture and context in devising responsive approaches to what all those harmed by the violence need.

Pennell and Kim (2010) open up interesting issues that are little aired in England. They are both uneasy about the reliance of domestic abuse and child welfare organisations on legal remedies to protect women and children and both are committed to identifying ways to engage culturally based groups – the family and community – in stopping family violence. They use the term 'family violence' to refer to violations that cut across generations and gender within family groups, that is the immediate family members, their relatives and other close connections. However, to effect family and community engagement, Kim seeks 'creative interventions' outside the state whereas Pennell seeks to 'widen the circle' of formal and informal supports. One seeks alternatives to law enforcement, the courts, and prisons, while the other seeks to elevate the leadership of the family and its community, while still exerting legal leverages to safeguard children and adults within the home (p 178).

Pennell's concern to 'widen the circle' identifies four main strategies or pathways for engaging family and community in supporting and protecting child and adult family members.

> These pathways are 'family leadership' that centralizes the role of the family in making and carrying out plans, 'inclusive planning' that involves different sides of the family in the process, 'cultural safety' that fosters a context in which family members can tap into their traditions in reaching resolutions, and 'community partnerships' that encourage local collaborations while seeking to achieve shared goals. (p 178)

Pennell's approach is located within restorative justice aspirations of bringing to bear the caring and knowledge of those harmed, those who committed the harm, and the wider community, so to build trust, heal the trauma and create the conditions for peace. It does not mean replacing the legal system but is a means of engaging and empowering communities to use the law to safeguard human rights. There is, however, a constant tension of aligning with state systems. 'Governments provide funds to services and access to people charged with offenses and at the same time limit the goals and shape the processes of organizations seeking to effect RJ' (p 179).

Pennell develops family group meetings with the authorisation of state agencies and Kim develops creative interventions under community auspices. Both emphasise the helpful role of the family unlike much of the discourse in domestic abuse circles. 'Family-centered' forums are where families and their networks are integral to decision making, without relinquishing state resources and protections. Child maltreatment has already been established and as a result the question is how to address it.

A key issue of course concerns having both perpetrators and survivors at the same meeting. A range of steps is put in place to support safety – the safety steps 'demonstrate concerted efforts by some child protection programmes to widen the circle and engage family and community as effectively as possible, and these efforts elicit positive responses from families. At the same time, the numerous steps required demonstrate how much effort must go into organising such planning forums under state sponsorship and the unease of many workers and their agencies with their liability if participants become violent or if the plans fail to protect the children' (p 185).

A crucial aspect of Pennell's work concerns that carried out with men who are abusive. A potential strategy for mitigating the recurrence of family violence is to support the men in assessing and managing their own risk to family members (Pennell, Rikard and Sanders-Rice, 2013). This is the aim of the Strong Fathers programme, which was developed and tested in North Carolina, a state in the south-eastern United States. The programme was a parenting group for men with a history of committing domestic abuse and whose families received child protection services.

The overarching framework of Strong Fathers moved away from crime-centred risk approaches to engage men in solution finding. Guided by this theory of change, the programme encouraged the men to specify their change goals, develop skills for reaching these goals, and reconstruct themselves as responsible fathers. The programme evaluation examined the extent to which the men, from their own perspective, attained their goals. The men's self-assessments were checked against state administrative data on child maltreatment and domestic abuse. Pennell et al suggest that Strong Fathers is a starting point for reinforcing responsible fathering, resolving the harms of family violence and its underlying causes, and restoring a sense of personhood. A really fundamental underpinning premise is how discrimination and oppression are so often reinforced by state services. Engaging men as agents of change in a way that is respectful is a first step. The men's testimonies suggest they struggle however in a society that offers highly restrictive messages about what it is to be a man, especially in relation to the economic provider role, and yet places serious obstacles in the way of achieving such goals.

The context for this work bears some relation to ours currently although there are of course significant differences between legal and policy contexts in the US and England. In the US, during the 1980s and 1990s, the application of legal interventions to the maltreatment of children, intimate partner violence, and immigration rose. As governments reduced their social supports to families and reporting of child abuse and neglect increased, the net for child protection widened. With limited resources and escalating referrals, child welfare became increasingly restricted to forensic investigations and child removal from home rather than supporting families in caring for their children. At the same time, domestic abuse agencies came to rely even more on the criminal justice system, despite their distrust of the police and the courts and their concerns about zero-tolerance policies leading to the dual arrest of couples.

Pennell and others consider these developments and the tensions they provoked and inhumanities exposed opened up spaces for less adversarial and more restorative processes. The limits of such approaches are, however, sharply posed by compatible attempts recently in England and we now explore these.

We have already noted the use FGCs in Leeds in the area of domestic abuse (see Sen et al, 2018). The evaluation found that the families who used the service were incredibly positive, and there was repeated evidence of children exercising their influence on plans, of women drawing strength from other women in their networks to assert their rights, and of men seeking to change their behaviour and make positive contributions to family plans.

However, despite highly skilled relational practice from coordinators and real determination from families, the service was still curtailed by mother-centric and risk-focused systems and routine practices.

The service could relatively easily assist women to build support networks and positively plan for their and their children's future. It demonstrated it could also help families arrive at safe plans for any contact between children and fathers, and support family networks to arrive at contingency plans (and these meetings included paternal and maternal family members). But the service struggled to hold FGCs where restorative outcomes were the aim – in essence where the FGC focused on men addressing the harms they had caused/were causing.

Existing systems are preoccupied by assessing whether a mother can keep her children safe, and changing the focus to how the harm the man presented could be addressed simply could not fit within existing processes. Ironically, for some children, arriving at plans to prevent further violence from the man would have been the most protective outcome but was the least possible outcome.

For many women the end result of current practices is a silencing, fearful of being found wanting as a mother and no safe space as a woman. As Solnit (2017: 19) notes: 'violence against women is often against our voices and our stories. It is a refusal of our voices, and what a voice means: the right to self-determination, to participation, to consent or dissent, to live and to participate, to interpret and narrate.' Such nuanced understandings appear not to be possible to develop in current systems – as the FGC examples demonstrate the dominant paradigm can hold back even well-resourced and skilfully implemented alternative approaches.

We hold out great hope for the evolution of restorative approaches in a way that engages with economic and social circumstances. But it is imperative that we locate such approaches within a different story.

A social model of protecting children: domestic abuse

A social model in this area asks academics, policy makers, their managers and practitioners to engage in very sophisticated and nuanced practices at a range of levels. It obliges the most careful attention be paid to individual stories of pain and trauma *and to* social understandings of inequalities and suffering and the shame associated with them. It is vital that either/or logics are eschewed. Thus we must engage with the complexity of *gendered* power relations, rather than simply coding gender as referring only to boys and men, and consider the dangers that are posed for all concerned by investments in models of masculinity *and* femininity that are clung to by precariously positioned and very vulnerable men and women.

Goldner et al's (1991) work in this area continues to be relevant. A feminist family therapist, Goldner works with couples, arguing that the consequences of studying 'the ambivalent paradoxical expressions and meanings of power in intimate relationships have led most feminists away from simplistic characterizations of victims and victimisers towards more complex views of power as a relational arrangement buttressed by the larger socio–political context of gender inequality but not reducible to it' (pp 64–5).

Overall, we would suggest a range of strategies is required, obliging attention to local and societal constructions of gender relations, the local and societal opportunities available to achieve lives of dignity and respect, and the complexities of individual life histories. It obliges attention to questions within the broader context of those identified in previous chapters as follows:

- What is expected of men in this society, in this neighbourhood?
- What do women want from or expect from their lives and loves?
- What kinds of fathering and mothering did you experience?
- Were such experiences unique to you growing up?
- What were the bits you felt were most unique to you?
- What inspired you as a young person?
- Where are the resources for you to be the kind of man/woman you want to be?

The current disconnect between the empirical work that traces the significant changes in everyday lives and the harms social workers must address reduces the relevance and potency of the profession's capacity to support change. By dealing with domestic abuse in isolation from a systematic analysis of changes in men's lives we risk reinforcing unsafe conditions for women and children. This short story of the men in one family illustrates some of these issues:

John is 65. He lives and worked in a community that was built around the local mine. He lost his job in late 1990s when the mine closed. Unlike most of his friends, he did find other work as an 'odd jobs' man until ill-health forced him to retire.

His son Stuart is 43. He worked down the mine with his dad for a couple of years before the pit closed and he went to the local college and trained as a chef. He set up his own catering business but the business struggled as the community dealt with the mine closure. He is currently working at the local hotel on a low-paid, short-term contract.

His son George is 21. He has just finished his course at a local university, graduating with a first class degree in business studies and is now thinking about moving to London where the opportunities open to him will be greater.

These stories attest to changing work landscapes in one region and how these are played out intergenerationally. These are not of course unique to that region. Understanding what such changes meant for a key aspect of men's sense of masculinity – the economic provider role – is vital. How have men like John and Stuart adapted? What have been the consequences intergenerationally of the shift from stable work organised around place and community? What about other aspects of men's identity? What has been gained and lost? What about connections to sources of attachment and meaning such as clubs, trade unions and choirs? Crucially, what has happened to the women in their lives, partners, sisters, daughters and granddaughters?

A piece of research engaged in by one of the authors suggests there are examples of work with young men in specific economic and social contexts that are not specifically focused on domestic abuse but that may hold out possibilities for this area of work (see Robb et al, 2015, Featherstone et al, 2016). Fifty young men engaging in a range of projects run by Action for Children and Working with Men shared their perspectives on what makes 'a good worker' and on the salience, or otherwise, of gender in supporting good relationships. The accounts from the young men highlighted the importance of feeling 'cared for' and receiving acts of care from workers. They stressed the importance of the individual worker and his or her qualities and valued opportunities to engage with those who had been through similar experiences or who came from the same kinds of geographical background as they did. While the young men rejected categorical understandings of their lives and experiences and were strongly wedded to individualised projects, the services they were engaged with were steeped in practices and understandings that certain groups of people (for example, marginalised men) or situations (for example, young men who had been in prison) needed reparative services and the opportunities to develop safer masculinities. It is possible that such practices and understandings made it possible for the young men to assert their individuality as they were indeed safe 'to be themselves' but this is speculation on our part.

A third of the young men lived in an area of the UK (the West of Scotland) that had been devastated by de-industrialisation and most lived in areas and/or families struggling with change, loss and deprivation. A further third who were Black and minority ethnic (BME) lived in a city, London, that was experiencing enormous changes in terms of economic and social changes with swathes of the city becoming increasingly out of reach to all but the most wealthy. As we have already noted, Frost and Hoggett (2008) argue for the importance of grasping the relationship between individual biographies and the social processes attached to such huge social changes. They highlight the importance of attending to feelings of loss, grief and melancholia to understand the experiences of those whose communities are destroyed by processes of urban modernisation, or those who are the powerless objects of economic and social restructuring.

A significant number of the young men we spoke to had experienced multiple losses within their own lives within such communities; mothers, fathers, grandparents as well as moves in care and into prison. Such losses were linked to physical and mental health inequalities and thus to wider processes as Frost and Hoggett (2008) suggest in their analysis. They note that experiences that have been forced on us rather than those we freely choose, those we face as powerless objects rather than as active agents, threaten to go beyond our capacity for thought and emotional processing. They argue that it is very damaging if we are not able to think about our experiences and make sense of them emotionally and intellectually. Indeed, in such circumstances, there are a number of very different possibilities for how we act/react. These include self-destructive behaviour (such as alcohol and substance misuse), behaviour that is damaging or harmful to places, and destructive and damaging behaviour towards others, including those more vulnerable.

We have noted elsewhere (Featherstone et al, 2016) that damaging constructions of masculinity fuel the issues for young men who have been constructed as risks to others and threats to the social order. Thus it can be hard for young men to lay claim to a language of pain, vulnerability and hurt. We also noted the lack of a language around structural inequality for them to access, growing up as they had in a highly unequal society with a neoliberal emphasis on risks and opportunities as individually generated and dependent on character or choice (Featherstone et al, 2014).

The practices of the workers were steeped in understandings of the damage that can be done by vulnerable young men's investment in 'hyper-masculinity'. Such hyper-masculinity can be defined as acts of aggression, violence, risk taking, substance misuse, drinking large amounts of alcohol and overt heterosexuality and homophobic language and behaviour. Practitioners worked with the young men on alternative futures and what can be described as 'safer' masculinities and transitions. They used a holistic strengths-based approach often within local centres where it was possible to get a warm drink and respite from a cold and lonely flat, help with job applications, emotional support with loss and pain, and where they were challenged on damaging and destructive sexist and abusive language and behaviours. Thus the young men were offered high support but also high challenge, obliging them to take responsibility for their behaviours and to 'do better'.

While not focused on domestic abuse, we consider there is much potential here to inform alternative approaches to those decontextualised programmes that focus on men solely as problems and on offering highly rational challenges to their 'faulty' thinking.

Concluding thoughts

Like all aspects of our project, domestic abuse poses enormous challenges, ironically perhaps, given that generally it has been understood as a social issue to be tackled on multiple levels. Feminists have fought very hard to challenge constructions that reduce it to a matter of individual psychology or relationship pathology and have rooted it in broader understandings of gendered power relations and in particular constructions of masculinity that emphasise men's sense of entitlement over women. However, we would argue this has translated into a risk-focused, highly individualised child protection paradigm and has too often resulted in responsibility being ascribed to women with men becoming the invisible risky 'other'.

It is an irony, indeed, that a paradigm that focuses on the individual has so often proved unable to offer anything other than the most socially reductive understandings and shied away from conversations about what is actually going on between men and women in specific places and spaces.

EIGHT

Crafting different stories: changing minds and hearts

Introduction

In this penultimate chapter we shift gear in order to think about how we might change the conversation on 'child protection'. We explore the specific issues of seeking to effect social change within a 'post-truth' climate and discuss how we might draw from work in social psychology, cognitive linguistics and the sociology of emotions to learn the craft of telling stories. It is hoped such stories might promote identification across divided sections of the population and key into and promote shared values, in order to develop a social model of protecting children.

In doing so we remain mindful of the quote with which we opened this book:

> Changing the story isn't enough in itself, but it has often been foundational to real changes. Making an injury visible and public is usually the first step in remedying it, and political change often follows culture, as what was long tolerated is seen to be intolerable, or what was overlooked becomes obvious. *Which means that every conflict is in part a battle over the story we tell, or who tells and who is heard.* (Solnit, 2016: xiv, emphasis added)

Who tells which stories and who is heard are political issues and we seek to offer some thoughts on how we can develop new kinds of 'politics' that support the telling of multiple stories by a range of constituencies in inclusive and respectful forums.

Navigating a post-truth landscape

In 2016, The *Oxford English Dictionary* selected 'post-truth' as its word of the year. Defined by the dictionary as an adjective 'relating to or denoting circumstances in which objective facts are less influential in shaping public opinion than appeals to emotion and personal belief', editors said that use of the term 'post-truth' had increased by around 2,000% in 2016 compared to the previous year (see Flood, 2016).

Post Brexit, Davies (2016) has noted that one of the complaints made most frequently by liberal commentators, economists and media pundits is that the referendum campaign was conducted without regard to 'truth'. He argues, however, that this was not quite right. It was more accurate to reflect that it was conducted without adequate regard to the 'facts'. To the great frustration of the Remain campaign, their 'facts' never caught on with the electorate, whereas Leave's 'facts' (most famously the £350m/week price tag of EU membership) did appear to be believed.

Davies (2016) explores the history and changing fortunes of the 'fact'. He draws on the work of Poovey, who noted that a new way of organising and perceiving the world came into existence at the end of the 15th century with the invention of double-entry book keeping. This new style of knowledge was that of *facts*, representations that seemed both context independent, but also able to flow between multiple contexts as required. The basis for this was that measures and methodologies were standardised, but then treated as apolitical, so the numbers could move around freely without challenge. In order for this to work, the infrastructure that produced 'facts' needed careful monitoring with rigorous gate keeping, ideally through centralisation in the hands of statistics agencies or elite universities.

Davies suggests 'facts' (such as statistics) survived as an authoritative basis for public and democratic deliberation for most of the 200 years following the French Revolution. But the politicisation of social sciences, metrics and policy administration mean currently that the 'facts' produced by official statistical agencies must compete with other conflicting 'facts'. The deconstruction of 'facts' has been partly fostered by varieties of postmodernism since the 1960s, but it is also an inevitable effect of the attempt to turn policy into a scientific exercise.

Davies argues that the attempt to reduce politics to a utilitarian science backfires, once the science becomes politicised. As was most obvious under New Labour, 'evidence-based policy' morphed into 'policy-based evidence'. Thus in the Brexit campaign, when the Remain camp appealed to their 'facts', they hoped that these would be judged as beyond politics and they operated under an illusion that the opinions of bodies such as the International Monetary Fund (IMF) might be viewed as 'independent'. This, in retrospect, seems extraordinary, given the now widespread recognition of the role economics as a discipline has played in supporting various political ideologies, most notably those that have resulted in a great deal of poverty and inequality and, as Davies notes, economics is now considered as anything but outside the fray of politics.

Davies argues we now live in a world of *data*. Instead of trusted measures and methodologies being used to produce numbers, they are produced by a vast array of means, to be analysed and interpreted for a variety of purposes, most often with selling us everything from shoes to ideas. He argues that risk modelling (using notions of statistical normality) was the defining research technique of the 19th and 20th centuries but that sentiment analysis is the defining one of the emerging digital era.

The implications for researchers, and particularly for those seeking to effect social change, are very wide ranging indeed. However, it has long been clear that hurling 'facts' in the form of statistics at people is likely to change very few minds. Evans (2017) highlights this clearly, drawing on his experience as a climate change activist arguing that it is stories, rather than facts and pie charts, that have the power to animate us and bring us together to change the world.

Featherstone (2016), drawing from framing theory, has begun to identify some of the key stories that have been dominant in relation to child protection over the decades. Organisations such as the New Economics Foundation, NSPCC and the Joseph Rowntree Foundation have also been using methodologies derived from framing theory to explore how different stories could be crafted on poverty, child abuse and neglect. In Chapter three we have identified some of the concerns around the use of framing theory; here we acknowledge these but also its possibilities and opportunities.

Framing our worlds: how and what?

George Lakoff (2014) is a cognitive linguist who has spent decades exploring the framing of public discourse in the US and advising advocacy groups and politicians on framing issues from a progressive perspective. Lakoff argues all too many progressives have been taught a false and outdated theory of reason, one in which framing, metaphorical thought and emotion play no role in rationality – this has led them to the view that the facts alone will set them free. 'Facts matter enormously, but to be meaningful, they must be framed in terms of their moral importance' (p xiv).

According to Lakoff (pp xi–xii) frames are mental structures that shape the way we see the world. They shape the goals we seek, the plans we make, the way we act and what counts as a good or bad outcome. Frames are part of what he calls the 'cognitive unconscious' – 'structures in our brains that we cannot consciously access, but know by their consequences' (p xii). In politics, frames shape social policies and the institutions we form to shape our policies. To change our frames is to change all of this. He argues that reframing is social change:

> When we successfully reframe public discourse, we change the way people see the world. We change what counts as common sense. Because language activates frames, new language is used for new frames.

Framing is not about coming up with clever slogans. Certain ideas have to be ingrained in us, developed over time consistently and precisely enough to create an accurate frame for our understanding. It is difficult to say things people are not ready to hear. Lakoff argues this is a problem of hypocognition – the lack of the overall neural circuitry that makes common sense of the idea and that fits the form of communication that one normally engages in. Slogans cannot overcome hypocognition – only sustained public discussion has a chance and that involves knowledge of the problem and a large-scale serious commitment to work for a change.

The world reflects our understandings through our actions, and our understandings reflect the world shaped by the frame-informed actions of ourselves and those of others. To function effectively in the world it helps to be aware of reflexivity, to be aware of what frames have shaped and are still shaping reality if you are going to intervene to make the world a better place.

A really crucial point made by Lakoff is that even when we are negating a frame, we are evoking it because the more we repeat a frame even if only to disagree with it, the stronger it gets. Thus, Lakoff counsels, when arguing against the other side in an argument, do not use their language. For example, he notes in a blog (2017) that in response to President Trump calling journalists 'enemies', journalists have resisted by using hashtags in social media campaigns such as #NotTheEnemy. He argues that adopting this hashtag is a big mistake. Rather, he counsels journalists instead to use a hashtag such as #ProtectTheTruth.

Lakoff argues that the most effective frames connect with people's values. Appealing to values increases the chance people will engage with and respond to what is said, because values are things we hold in common, that resonate at a deep emotional level. Furthermore, the more we appeal to a value, the stronger it becomes. The concern with values is vitally important. Researchers have identified a core set of values that are distributed differently in different types of societies. Intrinsic values cluster around empathy, care and are other oriented. Extrinsic values cluster around achievement, status and money. Values change and can be changed by a range of activities at cultural, political and economic levels.

The New Economics Foundation (NEF) used framing to explore 'the austerity story' promoted to such great effect by the Coalition Government after 2010. It is worth outlining this in some detail as it provides a vivid illustration of how a compelling story was crafted (see NEF, 2013: 8–11 for the analysis in detail).

Based on desk-based analysis of media debate and government communications, researchers at NEF identified seven core frames behind the austerity story, shaping the terms in which people think about the economy. Some of them were long-standing frames that the austerity story sought to reinforce, frames that have been developing over the last decades. Others were attempts to reframe the debate, and to directly change the way people thought about the economy.

The seven frames were as follows:

Dangerous debt

Debt, as a result of public spending, caused the economic crisis. The frame that sits behind this says debt is dangerous – something threatening and to be feared. This frame pre-dates the austerity story. Most people hold negative frames about debt. What the austerity story did is combine existing fears about debt with an understanding of what is wrong with the economy. This means that single words are likely to activate the frame: borrowing, debt, deficit, credit, national debt. These words have become associated with the dangerous debt frame in our minds, they remind us to be afraid of debt, that the national debt is too high and must be repaid.

Britain is broke

Frames are often metaphors and the austerity story repeatedly compared the UK and its economy to an individual household that had spent all its money. This was a frame that was used very successfully by Margaret Thatcher in the past. This metaphor makes thinking about the economy accessible because it compares it to something that is familiar to us all. If this frame is strongly held, presenting facts that suggest the national economy doesn't resemble a household's finances will be ignored, no matter how good these facts are, because they do not fit the frame.

Austerity is a necessary evil

Spending cuts are never presented as desirable but are presented as if, sadly, there is no alternative to them. This is a very powerful way to frame an argument, suggesting there is no choice to be made. NEF researchers argued this as being really central to the austerity story, the part that must be accepted to make the plot believable. Importantly, following Lakoff, opponents who argue against austerity by using arguments about the pain it causes and not challenging its necessity are not attacking this frame and are therefore likely to strengthen it.

Big bad government

Government is bad and it's too big. Framing government negatively has been a theme since the 1980s particularly, and is separate from issues of debt and spending. The austerity story blames government for building up debt, but it also blames it for interfering in people's lives, for rewarding the undeserving and impeding the proper functioning of the economy. The logic of this frame is clear, government is bad and the bigger government is, the worse that is for the economy.

This frame is embedded now after decades of usage.

Welfare is a drug

Drug addiction evokes its own frames, most of which are negative and to do with human weakness. Framing welfare negatively is long standing and by no means unique to the austerity story. The language of dependency activates this frame, as does talking about the weakness or recklessness of people on benefits.

Strivers and skivers

There are two kinds of people in Britain: strivers and skivers. Strivers go to work and play by the rules whereas skivers choose to be unemployed. This frame is deliberately divisive and 'othering': it invites people to self-identify as a striver, a good and respectable person, and frames those on benefits or out of work as lazy. Beneath it is the inference that strivers and skivers make a choice; they choose to contribute or to live off others' hard work. The frame is clearly being activated when words like skiver and scrounger are being used, but also with loaded terms that imply two types of people: 'hard-working families' suggests there are lazy families; 'those who work hard' reminds us that many do not work hard or even work at all; and 'genuine benefit claimants' implies large numbers of people claim benefits fraudulently. Using the language of choice, particularly to do with unemployment, also engages the frame.

Labour's mess

The austerity story blames the previous (Labour) government for almost all that is wrong with the economy. By framing the problems as Labour's mess, the Coalition reinforced itself as the hero in its own story, righting the wrongs created by others. Mess is an important part of this frame as it evokes chaos and ineptitude. Labour's mess is a term invoked regularly to activate this frame, as are references to 'the previous government' in connection with bad news about the economy, or talk of the deficit and spending.

Overall, the austerity story sets out clear frames for debates about the economy. Each frame tells its own story, which in turn fits into and reinforces the larger narrative. Each frame comes with its own language and metaphors which activate it in people's minds. The frames work on their own but they also support each other. Like all good and memorable stories, it has a plot, heroes and villains and a clear moral, is full of metaphors and very memorable and easily grasped.

By deconstructing the story NEF sought to identify the project that was being pursued by the then government, the chief architect of which was George Osborne, a well-known admirer of Margaret Thatcher. It is thus useful to be reminded of her views on the role of economic policy: '... it isn't that I set out on economic policies; it's that I set out really to change the approach, and changing the economics is the means of changing that approach. If you change the approach you really are after the heart and soul of the nation. Economics are the method; the object is to change the heart and soul' (Margaret Thatcher, quoted in Common Cause, 2010: 23).

As we identified, framing is concerned to strengthen certain values. In this case 'the austerity story' seeks to strengthen the values of self-discipline, independence, reciprocity, ambition and wealth (NEF, 2013).

We have used this work by NEF to deconstruct a story on child protection best articulated by Michael Gove, the then Minister for Education, in 2013 (see Featherstone, 2016):

> In too many cases, social work training involves idealistic students being told that the individuals with whom they will work have been disempowered by society. They

will be encouraged to see these individuals as victims of social injustice whose fate is overwhelmingly decreed by the economic forces and inherent inequalities which scar our society. This analysis is, sadly, as widespread as it is pernicious. It robs individuals of the power of agency and breaks the link between an individual's actions and the consequences. It risks explaining away substance abuse, domestic violence and personal irresponsibility, rather than doing away with them.

The quote from Mr Gove above fits with an old story about children, parents, abuse, neglect and the roles and responsibilities of the state and families that has been reinvigorated with some new twists added since 2010. It runs as follows:

1. Child protection is a specific activity that is largely concerned about stopping children dying or being harmed/neglected by their parents or carers.
2. Many parents and carers make dangerous or poor lifestyle choices. They choose violent men and/or to waste their money on drink and drugs.
3. Their lifestyles are aided and abetted by a dangerous and 'out-of-control' welfare system.
4. They are able to outwit gullible social workers who, though well meaning, are let down by social work educators.
5. These educators tell them not to blame or condemn parents, but rather to see them as victims of poverty or inequality.
6. But poverty and inequality have nothing to do with child abuse.
7. Social justice is about rescuing children from these feckless parents as early as possible and having them adopted.

This story has driven system change in England in recent years as well as informing what is researched and, indeed, what is not researched. The framing feeds into values identified above in relation to 'them and us', independence and self-discipline. It has a plot, heroes and villains and a moral.

Discussion of framing theory: perils and opportunities

[The] idea that people can be 'nudged' into new forms of behaviour by having their brains massaged in a certain way, is built on the premise that we are not rational beings to be engaged with. Its very foundation is the elite's view of us, not as people to be talked to, argued with and potentially won over, but problematic beings to be remade. (O'Neill, 2010, no page no.)

O'Neill is making extremely valid points here. Lakoff's work could support elites devising more and more sophisticated ways of framing that render human dialogue about pain, suffering, hope and change even more problematic to develop and ways of governing and discussing more and more opaque. And indeed a very powerful example of this was offered in Chapter three.

Moreover, Lakoff, in his emphasis on not repeating opponents' frames, has been accused of stoking the increasingly polarised politics of the US and of actively impeding possibilities for dialogue and problem solving about shared concerns. Jonathan Haidt (2012) is of interest in regard to this latter point. He is a social psychologist with a speciality in the psychology of morality and moral emotions. He too counsels against assumptions that relaying the facts or evidence will be enough to change people's minds. He argues that moral judgements arise not from reason but from intuition.

He argues that human minds are designed for 'groupish righteousness' and this makes it difficult but not impossible to connect with others who live in other matrices. He challenges those on the 'progressive' side to engage with conservative conceptions of morality. He argues that progressives fail to respect and appreciate moral values prized by conservatives: loyalty, authority and sanctity.

Alex Evans (2017), drawing from his experience of seeking to effect action on climate change, also counsels against the problems attached to campaigning that is based on 'enemy narratives'. He argues there is no need for narratives to have an enemy. He notes that human societies historically were rich in myths. Many myths were not about enemies to be conquered but were instead about a quest, or a challenge or overcoming some internal weakness. He argues that there is a myth gap today and this really matters. In a time of climate change, inequality and mass migration, there is an urgent need for new myths:

Tales of restoration are just about the most powerful and resonant kind there are – they speak directly to a profound yearning in all of us, an instinct that while the world may be broken, it can also be made right again, and that this may at some level be *what we are here to do*. (Evans, 2017: 74, emphasis in original)

Overall, we consider Lakoff's work has value, especially in the way as we showed, it has been used by NEF to deconstruct the frames used in the austerity story. But for our purposes it needs supplementing both by an understanding of the role of emotions that are invoked in relation to protecting children and also crucially by attention to developing processes concerned with expanding who tells what story and the forums in which stories are told in order to foster identification and solidarity and 'democratise' the storytelling in child protection.

As Warner (2015) notes, politicians in their involvement with child protection have been much more concerned with the dead than the living. She draws from the work of Arlie Hochschild (2002), who argued there is an emotional regime which is a structure that always exists but is rarely seen: 'The emotional regime includes a set of taken-for-granted feeling rules (rules about how we imagine we should feel) and framing rules (rules about the way we should see and think). Together these rules shape how we see and feel about everyday reality' (Hochschild, 2002: 118). Hochschild noted, for example, that after 9/11 new feeling rules concerning blame, fear and suspicion emerged with a new emotional stratification system in which different groups from before became targets of suspicion and fear.

This analysis, according to Warner, highlights the power that political leaders have to become 'feeling legislators', particularly over events that evoke deep social anxieties such as the deaths of children from abuse and neglect. The responses to such deaths have resulted in quite significant shifts in policy and practice, not just in the UK, but also in other countries (see the edited collection by Gilbert, Parton and Skiveness, 2011).

Warner (2015) highlights how stories about the deaths of children are caught up in the politics–media–politics cycle, in which politicians can speak for others and reflect or generate particular collective emotions – politicians act as emotional envoys on behalf of others: 'Political leaders are instrumental in telling us how to think and feel about child deaths but more importantly, who we should feel angry at and who should feel ashamed' (p 158). The stories support powerful narratives about particular groups and the emotions that attach to them often feeding into and promoting emotions of disgust and contempt about the Other.

Individual stories of child deaths at the hands of their parents or carers become the 'common sense' of child protection, with no space for other more socially disruptive stories or indeed for the evidence that such deaths are very rare and in long-term decline. As Pritchard and Williams (2010) note, the kinds of child deaths that exercise the media and politicians are becoming rarer. Jutte et al (2015) also note that the numbers of children dying as a result of homicide or assault are in long-term decline. In 2013, the rate of deaths due to assault and undetermined intent in Northern Ireland was 5.6 per million, followed by 3.8 per million in England and Wales and 3.5 per million in Scotland. The rate has declined in all four nations since the 1980s – by 59% in Scotland, 48% in Northern Ireland and 60% in England and Wales. By contrast, the numbers of children dying as a result of poverty and associated preventable issues are significant especially when compared with other more equal countries.

Wolfe et al (2014) note that comparing how children fare in different countries shows that children in the UK are among the more deprived in Western Europe. This is reflected in mortality rates; there is a higher mortality rate among children under five years old who live in countries with a high proportion of deprived households. The lowest mortality rates are in the Nordic countries, with the lowest proportions of deprived households (see also Viner et al, 2014). Wolfe et al (2014) note that every year, an estimated 2,000 additional children die in the UK compared to the best performing country in their comparative study, Sweden, a much more equal society than the UK with far less poverty. Their research showed that over half of the deaths in childhood occur during the first year of a child's life and are strongly influenced by pre-term delivery and low birth weight; with risk factors including maternal age, smoking and disadvantaged circumstances. Suicide remains a leading cause of death in young people in the UK, and the number of deaths due to intentional injuries and self-harm have not declined in 30 years. After the age of one, injury is the most frequent cause of death; over three quarters of deaths due to injury in the age bracket of 10–18-year-olds are related to traffic incidents. Poorer children are much more likely to live in more dangerous areas and accidents generally are more common in poorer households (see Featherstone et al, 2016).

But 'facts' such as those cannot be framed currently and thus cannot be heard – they do not fit within a narrative of individual culpability and responsibility.

Much of this is possible because of the amount of distancing that goes on in contemporary societies (Warner, 2015). A key insight from the work on the consequences of the growth in inequalities in societies such as ours concerns how distances between groups are intensified, including between social workers and their service users. Within the last decades, under both Conservative and Labour administrations, greater distances emerged between individuals, groups and communities; these were physical and psychological and affected everyone. Featherstone et al argued that these processes of distancing contributed to a breakdown in feelings of solidarity and commonality in the face of vulnerability and adversity. This distancing has had pernicious effects on the relationship between child and family social work and families (Featherstone et al, 2014).

Crafting different stories and opening up spaces for such stories to be told and heard involves moving into and occupying different emotional and physical spaces. In the next section we reflect on some of the issues that emerged from the adoption enquiry, which we have discussed previously, where such spaces were developed (Featherstone et al, 2018).

"I thought you would hate me"

> Words bring us together, and silence separates us, leaves us bereft of the help or solidarity or just communion that speech can solicit or elicit. (Solnit, 2017: 10)

There are few issues in child protection in the UK (and particularly but by no means exclusively in England) that prompt emotions such as shame, fear and anger so strongly as adoption. It also silences people and emotions. Here we offer some reflections on a process we developed as part of an enquiry into adoption commissioned by the British Association of Social Workers (BASW). As part of a range of methods used, we convened seminars in different parts of the UK in a variety of meeting places and invited birth parents, adoptive parents, adult adoptees, social workers, managers, academics and legal personnel to come together. It is important to note that these were not matched; the birth parents, adoptive parents, adoptees were not part of each other's families and the social workers were not those involved in the adoption. Four such meetings involved a mix of birth parents, adopters, adoptees and social workers. Two others involved social workers and their managers only and one did not include any birth parents. The meetings involved between 15 and 30 people and included eating together and small-group discussions with limited input by the organisers.

The methodology used drew loosely from that used in a previous initiative The Care Inquiry (2013). A series of 'ground rules' were developed to guide the conduct of the events and emphasised the importance of respecting confidentiality, listening without interruption and allowing the articulation of multiple perspectives respectfully. While the process and findings are explored in greater detail elsewhere (see

Featherstone et al, 2018). And here we explore how dialogue across 'divides' appeared to open up new understandings, identify future opportunities for co-production and promote a degree of identification between groups who are often constructed in opposition.

"I thought you would hate me" was a statement uttered by an adoptive mother to a birth mother. This statement referenced hate in the abstract; they were not known to each other before the event. Rather the adoptive mother assumed that any birth mother would hate her. Their discussion together, alongside others in the group, highlighted, however, their sense of shared purpose as the birth mother explained how important it was for her to feel her child was being cared for well. The pain of loss was eased in such circumstances, she noted, and, conversely, the pain of loss was intensified immeasurably if it was felt that adoptive parents were not able to love and care for their children. The emotional perils of zero-sum thinking were highlighted here as well as a clear sense of identification built as parents who want the best for children.

A really important aspect was where birth parents felt able to tell their stories. In two events parents with learning difficulties not only told stories of their experiences, but also offered concrete ideas for how they and others in their situations could be helped, and participants were introduced to a world they did not necessarily know about. For example, parents with learning difficulties highlighted how they were developing training resources for professionals, rooted in their experiences of what is needed to engage with how they learn and develop and what is required for services to really work with them as partners in caring safely for their children.

A professional from the third sector explained how working with a group of mothers living apart from their children over a number of years had led to the group now being involved in the training of prospective adopters, especially in relation to the importance of sustaining letter box contact. The mothers also were involved in social work education locally. Again, this offered the possibility of new understandings to other participants and also access to ideas about how they might develop their services further.

As has been documented, feeling silenced becomes an overriding experience for birth parents throughout the process leading up to, and following, adoption. Many are living with very high levels of loss, grief and shame. One mother's account of literally not being able to tell anyone of her situation is sobering. When going through child protection processes, she talked of not being able to tell the worker at the Citizen's Advice Bureau even though she desperately needed advice on benefit entitlements. When her children were adopted she could not talk to anyone and it was only through developing links with others on social media that non-shaming ways of sharing became available to her.

Butler (2004) explores whose lives are able to be grieved for and who is judged a legitimate griever. In obliging us to embrace the stranger or the 'Other', Butler draws attention to inclusion and exclusion in the very notion of who is considered human. She therefore opens up possibilities for rigorous painful conversations and questions. Who can be heard? Whose suffering can be grieved for? Who is left out in the narratives that predominate?

Adoptive parents and adoptees can also feel silenced as a result of the 'happy ever after' narrative that attends adoption, especially in the careless rhetoric of politicians. In the seminars, such processes were challenged and shared understandings of how love and loss, pain and joy, can coexist for all concerned. It would be cavalier to infer that the seminars were easy to be part of or that they automatically led to solidarity or a sense of shared purpose. But feedback and our own observations would suggest the following:

- Emotional and intellectual discomfort was inevitable.
- For a number this allowed or reinforced feelings of doubt about how current systems operate.
- For others it promoted feelings of empathy with all involved in adoption and a reaching out to perspectives they had not hitherto considered.

For us as the organisers, it highlighted the limited opportunities there are in our current arrangements for dialogue to occur in spaces that are not marked by coercion, shame and blame. We consider such opportunities are crucial to develop in future change. Family Group Conferences have emerged to challenge and redress problematic processes in relationships between the services and families. There is a need to think further about how dialogue can be expanded, including with politicians (see Warner, 2015).

Concluding thoughts

As Tobis (2013: xxvi) notes, Americans declare their concern for poor children by supporting a massive system to report abuses and remove children from their families, rather than a programme that would help struggling families by improving the difficult environments in which they live and reducing the stresses in the home that contribute to abuse and neglect. Surveys of public opinion in the UK offer a more nuanced picture. While it is correct that the most popular response to questions about what should be done is to remove children, the second most common response, which has increased in popularity in recent years, is to tackle poverty (Bentley et al, 2015).

Throughout this book we have been developing the building blocks for new stories to be told that builds on that second response. An overarching narrative goes something like this:

- Currently there are inequalities in children's chances of living safely within their families.
- These inequalities are directly related to deprivation and other forms of inequality such as in physical and mental health.
- Anti-poverty strategies need to be joined up with safeguarding strategies locally and nationally.
- The social determinants of many of the harms experienced by individuals and within families need to be recognised, understood and tackled.
- Social and collective strategies need to be integrated with practices directed at individual families.
- To protect children and promote their welfare we need to re-focus services on the contexts in which they live with their families.

This chapter has identified a variety of intellectual tools to support this project and has called for the expansion of spaces within which such a story can be developed further and heard by multiple audiences. It is vital that the values associated with such a story – fairness, care, empathy and solidarity – are recognised explicitly and championed overtly.

NINE

Concluding thoughts

Introduction

> Hope is an embrace of the unknown and the unknowable, an alternative to the certainty of both optimists and pessimists. Optimists think it will all be fine without our involvement; pessimists adopt the opposite position; both excuse themselves from acting. It is the belief that what we do matters even though how and when it may matter, who and what it may impact, are not things we can know beforehand. (Solnit, 2016: xii)

We are neither optimists nor pessimists and offer our contribution in the belief that *what we do* does indeed matter. Our premise is that we need to 'do differently' as we watch the year-on-year rise in the numbers of children being removed from their families of origin, and the translation of stories of need and trouble into categories of risk and shame.

In this conclusion we note that, in order to do differently, we need bigger conversations than hitherto. These must involve those from a range of endeavours and disciplines and all those concerned with, and impacted by, child protection. We also explore some possibilities for democratising conversations more generally.

Our new story is very different, and shifting paradigms is a complex business. We know we have a considerable distance to travel with these ideas. It may be that only some can take hold initially and we must think longer term about the underpinning changes needed. Nor do we think that we have a route map for the way forward, instead we have a desire for different conversations. Practitioners, families, academics and researchers have more to contribute than we are able to, but we hope we have stimulated an opening discussion based on a new story set out in the preceding chapter and repeated here:

- Currently there are inequalities in children's chances of living safely within their families.
- These inequalities are directly related to deprivation and other forms of inequality such as in physical and mental health.
- Anti-poverty strategies need to be joined up with safeguarding strategies locally and nationally.
- The social determinants of many of the harms experienced by individuals and within families need to be recognised, understood and tackled.
- Social and collective strategies need to be integrated with humane practices directed at individual families.
- To protect children and promote their welfare we need to re-focus services on the contexts in which they live with their families.

Let's talk

Talking across disciplines

Throughout the book, we have highlighted the need to make links with the scholarship on poverty and inequality and the psycho-social implications for children, young people, families and the wider society. We will not rehearse these arguments again but rather concentrate on an associated literature emerging that might be of help in reflecting on why protecting children is too often associated with a frightening state and what can be done about it.

In his book Peston (2017: 26) asks: why is trust in so many of the institutions and people who have run things for years at an all-time low, among the public, though not among the elite? He notes the findings from an annual survey of 28 countries that, in 2017, there has been an unprecedented collapse in trust among the 'mass of people' in government, the media, business and non-governmental organisations, with the gap largest in the UK and the US. Because those engaged in child protection often feel victimised and blamed, there has been inadequate understanding of, and reflection on, the evidence that they are perceived as part of a remote, frightening and alienating state/establishment.

This perception has been a long time in the making but the causes have not, we would suggest, been rigorously interrogated in terms of the links with marginalisation and deprivation. There has been too much reliance on analyses that highlight the role of the media in the demonisation of social work in particular. However, this appears an inadequate analysis when considered carefully. Surely, the logic of such an analysis is that social work practitioners are too incompetent to be feared. Our research with young people and their families suggests, however, that fear of an authoritarian and neglectful state is often to be found among those who experience racism and oppression and feel alienated and disconnected. This was particularly highlighted for us, over a decade ago now, through research with young men mainly from Black, Asian and minority ethnic (BAME) backgrounds on their interactions with social care services when becoming fathers (Featherstone and White, 2005). The young men recounted their perceptions of a state that was only interested in them if they suspected them of failing to meet their child support obligations or of being involved in domestic abuse. They did not see the state as *for* them or interested *in* them as equal citizens. For example, they did not consider that their support needs, as fathers, received adequate recognition. Similarly a study within a highly deprived community as part of the Child Welfare Inequalities Project revealed that, even when individual encounters had been highly positive, the shared narrative was one of fear and distrust of children's services. The sense of disconnect between positive experiences of an individual social worker and community antipathy towards the agency the social worker is employed by needs rigorous examination if new relationships are to be built.

This disconnect between individual experiences and communal folklore is also evident in many current policy analyses. Currently responses are often framed through 'underdog/underclass' binaries. As Sayer (2017) points out, focusing just on social determinants can allow social policy scholars to avoid uncomfortable community concerns about certain individuals and their behaviours. Equally, focusing on the pathologies of individuals/families with harmful behaviours allows broader policy and political questions to be sidelined. This type of moral muddle was evident in the narratives from the social workers who were the subject of Morris et al's research (2018a). While the underclass narrative was strongly evident, social workers also offered empathetic analyses of the impact of poverty and deprivation on family lives. As Sayer suggests in phrasing that is very pertinent to social workers: 'The difficulty for social scientists is how to acknowledge that anti-social and self-destructive behaviour does happen, while highlighting the structural features of society that produce poverty, inequality and insecurity' (2017: 163). We suggest if we are to get widespread engagement with, and investment in, what is needed to protect children, then more reliable allies need to be sought than those who simply adopt defended positions within polarising debates. In social work, talking about the relationship between child abuse, neglect and poverty is currently framed by notions of reinforcing or avoiding stigmatising or oppressive generalisations. But, accepting that poverty means it is more likely that children may be harmed means the societal and individual value of reducing child and family poverty becomes clearer. Poverty is a child protection matter and social work needs a conversation about what this means for our knowledge base and everyday practices.

Talking with wider members of the public

In her ground-breaking study on lay people's understandings of neglect, Williams (2017) found that participants were dissatisfied with the narrow child protection definitions of neglect that were on offer, and deeply suspicious of the way in which they believed professionals would respond to neglect-related concerns. For the participants, neglect was a far broader and more complex issue than its position as a subset of child maltreatment allows. She argued that to address these very different constructions of child neglect required a range of services, focused not simply or even predominantly on child protection, but more importantly on child and family welfare and support to assist parents and communities to meet the needs of children within them.

She noted that categories such as 'child neglect' are open to multiple interpretations and diverse investments and that democratisation of the conversation requires engagement with complexity. It also requires acknowledgment of different interests and power relations.

We are concerned that there are insufficient mechanisms to engage the public and, moreover, policy developments in relation to opening up debates about definition and understandings are poorly developed. Indeed, there seems to be a move away from this type of approach. For example, Williams noted that Local Safeguarding Children Boards had been urged to recruit lay members representing the local community as a means both of accessing lay support and disseminating expert understandings on child protection work. This looks a rather top-down and paternalistic brief but even this brief appears imperilled by recent government developments restricting the remit and membership of such boards (DfE, 2016).

Where else can debate be encouraged and promoted? There are a variety of forums such as social media. This can ensure ideas and research papers are circulated widely and accessibly but it can also encourage soundbites and divisiveness. Indeed, it can add to what feels like a frenetic disputatious 'market place' of ideas, proposals and views, with people shouting across and past each other and contributing to what Jonathan Haidt (2012) has called 'groupish righteousness', thus entrenching divisions between people who all care deeply about the protection of children but are stuck in often very oppositional silos about what that means and, moreover, convinced that they have a monopoly on the morally correct way to proceed. We are anxious not to add to this although it is inevitable that we will do so to some extent.

Talking with those who experience services

Families have gained skills in dealing with substantive issues, for example in parenting in difficult conditions or in surviving and recovering from harmful encounters. For many this knowledge is painfully accrued but invaluable:

> 'At first, you just think it is all dangerous. At first, you think you have got to find him. You never find him, the police never find him; nobody finds him. It is real practical ... You have to keep adjusting what you are doing. We have licked it virtually, the running now. That has been successful, with the help of XXX but also with our own knowledge. Your own knowledge builds up. That is another thing that agencies need to understand, is that parents build up knowledge of what they are doing as well, so that you get to use every day things differently.'

They have built up an unparalleled knowledge of the range of welfare systems and services, and well-honed navigation skills. Routine opportunities to meet and collectively share this knowledge and these skills are rare. As other chapters make clear, positioning families as 'toxic' results in anxieties that collaboration between families is a means of compounding harm.

Obvious future possibilities present themselves. These can include peer support, co-construction of services, co-commissioning and joint service evaluation to name but a few. However, as those engaged in shifting cultures and practices towards more humane collaborative approaches know, even with the best of intentions the existing system design and cultures hamper progress.

But noting the potential here is important, the skills and the knowledge held by families can be utilised through a process of co-production to arrive at transformative approaches that function at the levels of practice, service design and policy, and internationally examples have emerged that offer rich learning.

Bridging the divides within social work itself

One of the most problematic features of policy developments in recent decades was the splitting of children's and adults' services by New Labour. This has led to numerous interface difficulties for those seeking to negotiate bewildering and complex services. But it has also resulted in quite different trajectories being taken by different parts of social work and inadequate attention being paid to learning from each other.

Our engagement with a social scientifically informed social model, which derives from and is influential in adult services, has made us conscious of the ways in which children's services have become locked into a really unhelpful paternalistic and protectionist paradigm, by contrast, certainly, with some developments in mental health services. This is exemplified by the findings we outlined in the Introduction in relation to the lack of a human rights discourse in relation to adoption, and child protection more generally, by contrast again with mental health, where there appears to be robust discussion about the contours of human rights-based practice.

We have noted how relationship-based practice has emerged, particularly in children's social work, and seems to be promoted often as the means by which practitioners can navigate a really complex landscape. We welcome this but see it as too narrowly focused on the professional/service user relationship. Again, we note more evidence in adult services, especially in mental health services, of the importance of networks and communities to recovery and flourishing. Another area, of course, is co-production, which is scarcely on the agenda in children's services as we have noted repeatedly.

We do not seek to romanticise developments in areas such as mental health – we know that these are very uneven – but the direction of conceptual travel and, in some cases, practice seems hopeful to us.

Taking the next steps

Choices and challenges for national policy makers

Place *inequalities at the centre of discussions* about protection for children, moving away from the dominant narrative of preventing child abuse tragedies (which is unattainable) towards a serious holistic approach to support that reduces the multiple, intersecting harms that children suffer.

What might this look like? Some examples we would suggest here are:

- embed and routinise the gathering on data on the economic and social circumstances of families whose children become looked after;
- join the dots between different types of inequality: health, educational and so on;
- take regional inequalities seriously;
- decentralise resources and decision making;
- recognise and address the ways in which deprivation drives demand for services and that regional inequalities are compounded and reinforced by Westminster actions currently.

Understand poverty as a child protection matter. In so doing broader and sustainable policies become possible that can provoke and support critical dialogue between families, communities and policy makers and bring to the fore the themes of redistribution and recognition.

Start conversations and build alliances that reach across social and cultural divides and that challenge all (policy makers, professionals and families) to begin a process of democratisation of the support of children and families.

Explore and expose the assumptions underpinning policy developments, *using the lens of children's rights.* The deficit model of child protection restricts the growth of policy initiatives that are capable of embedding rights and responsibilities, leaning instead too heavily on punitive reductionist interventions. It is vital that a holistic approach to rights is developed, that moves away from the neoliberal ethos underpinning individualist rescue models towards understandings that promote relational autonomy.

Seek to start conversations about how *open and non-shaming forms of dialogue* about raising children and young people are developed and fostered, generating an understanding of children as relational beings not islands that can be cut adrift. The role of national politicians is vital here and the track record is decidedly problematic, especially in recent decades (see Warner, 2015 and Chapter eight).

Social work academics and researchers too have a critical role to play in driving forward conversations that ask different questions of policy makers and raise the prospect of alternative understandings. Why, for example, is no data gathered by governments on the family circumstances of the children who become looked after? Why is there not robust longitudinal research on children's life chances, including their chances of being involved with child protection services? Why the lack of join up between research on educational inequalities, health inequalities and inequalities in child protection intervention rates? Why are issues such as drug and alcohol addiction so often researched as if they have no social determinants, with the main focus of research on techniques for individual interventions? How can we develop and support robust interdisciplinary research on individual stories of pain, loss and trauma that are sensitive to the intergenerational psycho-social contexts in which they are nested?

Challenges and choices at the level of the local state

In terms of challenges, OFSTED and outsourcing have become central mechanisms for shame and the fear of making a mistake has formed a backdrop to any developments. This fear is ever present and alerts us to the importance of building structures and processes to hold the risk and not retreat into 'unsafe certainty'.

The local state can act as an incubator for innovation in ways national state apparatus often cannot, and can translate notions of deliberative democracy into concrete opportunities for change. We have talked of the need to understand the child, the family, the community and the relational nature of children's well-being; engaging in different ways with local communities (be they determined by place, identity or experience) moves us on from the limits of decontextualised expert interventions that are often physically and emotionally remote from communities. As before, we can suggest themes and useful starting points but we recognise that these are just that, only a start.

In order to democratise approaches *build forums* to bring people together to support and promote the safe care and flourishing of children and young people in the community, so that the protective and supportive impulses of wider community members can be harnessed, and all those (including local practitioners) with expertise can inform service commissioning.

The level of investigative scrutiny of the poorest communities creates scars that need healing. *Create spaces for open dialogues* to talk about system abuses and injustices and to surface the stories of services that circulate within and about communities. This will give attention to the kinds of reparative and compensatory mechanisms needed for those who have suffered multiple traumas and systemic injustices

This includes building up knowledge about family incomes, work, and housing needs for example. This knowledge should be a core tenet of planning, designing and commissioning responses, not a backdrop that may or may not be acknowledged in service design. Thinking critically about how families and neighbourhoods inform service design pays attention to what families say they need to care adequately for their children, how safe they perceive their environment and what formal and community-based support services are there for children, young people and their families (and how families experience and use these services).

Concluding remarks

We would like to end on a hopeful note and have turned once again to Solnit's (2017: 18) profound and inspired arguments, which help us to understand and challenge the injustices of our society:

> Who is heard and who is not defines the status quo. Those who embody it, often at the cost of extraordinary silences with themselves, move to the centre; those who embody what is not heard or what violates those who rise on silence are cast out. By redefining whose voice is valued, we redefine our society and its values.

After Mary Richmond, Briskman (2013) argues for social workers to be 'courageous ethnographers', bearing witness to harm and the policies and processes that perpetuate injustice, and draws on the concept of 'moral outrage' to argue that the translation of personal distress into public issues is at the heart of the political project of social work (Williams and Briskman, 2015).

We offer this book as a contribution to redefining whose voices are valued in protecting children. It is a plea to root our practices in the voices and experiences of those who are struggling to live, love and care in conditions which make it difficult to do so with dignity and respect.

References

Allen, G. (2011a) *Early intervention: next steps*, London: Cabinet Office.

Allen, G. (2011b) *Early intervention: smart investment, massive savings*, London: Cabinet Office.

Allen, G. and Duncan Smith, I. (2009) *Early intervention: good parents, great kids, better citizens*, London: Centre for Social Justice and the Smith Institute, http://www.1001criticaldays.co.uk/buildinggreatbritonsreport.pdf.

All Party Parliamentary Group for Conception to Age 2: The First 1001 Days (2015) – *Building Great Britons*, https://plct.files.wordpress.com/2012/11/building-great-britons-report-conception-to-age-2-feb-2015.pdf.

Audit Commission (1994) *Seen but not heard: co-ordinating community child Health and social services for children in need*, London: HMSO.

Baldwin, M. (2009) 'Authoritarianism and the attack on social work', in Ferguson, I. and Lavalette, M. (eds) *Social Work After Baby P: Issues Debates and Alternative Perspectives*, Liverpool: Liverpool Hope University.

Bales, S.N. (2004) *Making the public case for child abuse and neglect prevention*, Washington, DC: FrameWorks Institute.

Banks, S. (2016) 'Everyday ethics in professional life: social work as ethics work', *Ethics and Social Welfare*, vol 10, no 1, pp 35–52.

Barlow J. and Axford, N. (2014) 'Giving children a better start in life: from science to policy and practice', *Journal of Children's Services*, vol 9, no 2, pp 188–90.

Barlow, C. and Calam, R. (2011) 'A public health approach to safeguarding in the 21st century', *Child Abuse Review*, vol 20, no 4, pp 238–55.

Barnes, C. (1991) *Disabled People in Britain and discrimination: a case for anti-discrimination legislation*, London: C. Hurst & Co.

Barnes, C. (2012) 'Understanding the social model of disability', in Watson, N., Roulstone, A. and Thomas, C. (eds) *Routledge Handbook of Disability Studies*, London: Routledge.

Barnes, M. and Morris, K. (2008) 'Strategies for the prevention of social exclusion: an analysis of the Children's Fund' *Journal of Social Policy*, vol 37, no 2, pp 251–70.

Bauman, Z. (2007) *Liquid times: living in an age of uncertainty*, Cambridge: Polity Press.

Beers, C.W. (1921) *The Mental Hygiene Movement*, New York: Longmans, Green and Co.

Belsky, J. and van Ijzendoorn, M.H. (2015) 'What works for whom? Genetic moderation of intervention efficacy', *Development and Psychopathology*, vol 27, pp 1–6.

Beresford, P. (2002) 'Thinking about "mental health": towards a social model', *Journal of Mental Health*, vol 11, no 6, pp 581–4.

Beresford, P. and Carr, S. (eds) (2012) *Social care, service users and user involvement*, London: JKP.

Beresford, P., Nettle, M. and Perring, R. (2010) *Towards a social model of madness and distress: exploring what service users say*, York: Joseph Rowntree Foundation.

Bevan, G. and Hood, C. (2006) 'What's measured is what matters: targets and gaming in the English public health care system', *Public Administration*, vol 84, no 3 pp 517–38.

Bilson, A. and Martin, K. (2016) 'Referrals and child protection in England: one in five children referred to Children's Services and one in nineteen investigated before the age of five', *British Journal of Social Work*, Advance Access, published on May 24, 2016. DOI: 10.1093/bjsw/bcw054.

Bilson, A., Featherstone, B. and Martin, K. (2017) 'How child protection's "investigative turn" impacts on poor and deprived communities', *Family Law Journal*, vol 47, no 4, pp 416-419.

Boyce, W.T., Sokolowski, M.B. and Robinson, G.E. (2012) 'Toward a new biology of social adversity', *Proceedings of the National Academy of Sciences*, vol 109, supplement 2, pp 17143–8.

Brandon, M., Sidebotham, P., Bailey, S., Belderson, P., Hawley, C., Ellis, C. and Megson, M. (2012) *New learning from serious case reviews: a two year report for 2009–2011,* Research Report DFE-RR226, London: DfE.

Brewer, C. and Lait, J. (1980) *Can social work survive?* London: Temple Smith.

Bridges, J.W. (1928) 'The mental hygiene movement', *The Public Health Journal*, vol 19, pp 1–8.

Briskman, L. (2013) 'Courageous ethnographers or agents of the state: challenges for social work', *Critical and Radical Social Work*, vol 1, no 1, pp 51–66.

Broadhurst, K. and Holt, K. (2010) 'Partnership and the limits of procedure: prospects for relationships between parents and professionals under the New Public Law outline', *Child and Family Social Work*, vol 15, no 1, pp 97–106.

Broadhurst, K., Alrouch, B., Yeend, E., Harwin, J., Shaw, M., Pilling, M., Mason, C. and Kershaw, S. (2015a) 'Connecting events in time to identify a hidden population: birth mothers and their children in recurrent care proceedings in England', *British Journal of Social Work*, vol 45, no 8, pp 2241–60.

Broadhurst, K., Shaw, M., Kershaw, S., Harwin, J., Alrouh, B., Mason, C. and Pilling, M. (2015b) 'Vulnerable birth mothers and repeat losses of infants to public care: is targeted reproductive health care ethically defensible?' *Journal of Social Welfare and Family Law*, vol 37, no 1, pp 84–98.

Brown, L. and Walter, T. (2013) 'Towards a social model of end-of-life care', *The British Journal of Social Work*, vol 44, no 8, pp 2375–90.

Brown, R. and Ward, H. (2013) *Decision-making within the child's timeframe*, London: DfE.

Bruer, J.T. (1999) *The myth of the first three years*, New York: The Free Press.

Bunting, L., McCartan, C., McGhee, J., Bywaters, P., Daniel, B., Featherstone, B. and Slater, T. (2017) 'Trends in child protection across the UK – a comparative analysis', *British Journal of Social Work*, Advance Access, published on 17 October 2017, DOI: 10.1093/bjsw/bcx102.

Burchardt, T. (2004) 'Capabilities and disability: the capabilities framework and the social model of disability', *Disability & Society*, vol 19, no 7, pp 735–51.

Burman, E., Smailes, S.L. and Chantler, K. (2004) '"Culture" as a barrier to service provision and delivery: domestic violence services for minoritized women', *Critical Social Policy*, vol 24, no 3, pp 332–57.

Butler, J. (2004) *Precarious life: the powers of mourning and violence*, London: Verso.

Bywaters, P., Bunting, L., Davidson, G., Hanratty, J., Mason, W., McCartan, C. and Steils, N. (2016) *The relationship between poverty, child abuse and neglect: an evidence review*, York: Joseph Rowntree Foundation.

Bywaters, P., Brady, G., Bunting, L., Daniel, B., Featherstone, B., Jones, C., Morris, K., Scourfield, J., Sparks, T. and Webb, C. (2018) 'Inequalities in English child protection practice under austerity: a universal challenge?' *Child and Family Social Work*, vol 23, no 1, pp 53–61.

Callaghan, J.E., Alexander, J.H. and Fellin, L.C. (2016) 'Children's embodied experience of living with domestic violence: "I'd go into my panic, and shake, really bad"', *Subjectivity*, vol 9, no 4, pp 399–419.

Carey, M. (2014) 'The Fragmentation of social work and social care: some ramifications and a critique', *British Journal of Social Work*, vol 45, no 8, pp 2406–22.

Carpenter, M. (2009) 'The capabilities approach and critical social policy: lessons from the majority world?', *Critical Social Policy*, vol 29, no 3, pp 351–73.

Caulkin, S. (2016) 'Everything you know about management is wrong', in Pell, C., Wilson, R. and Lowe, T. (eds) *Kittens are evil: little heresies in public policy*, Axminster: Triarchy.

Chakraborty, A. (2017) 'Foreword', in Davies, W. (ed) *The limits of neoliberalism: authority, sovereignty and the logic of competition*, London: Sage.

Chard, A. and Ayre, P. (2010) 'Managerialism – at the tipping point', in Ayre, P. and Preston-Shoot, M. (eds) *Children's services at the crossroads*, Lyme Regis: Russell House.

Chief Secretary to the Treasury (2003), *Every child matters*, Cmnd 5860, London: The Stationery Office.

Child Welfare Inequalities Project (2017) *Identifying and understanding inequalities in child welfare intervention rates: comparative studies in four UK countries. Briefing Paper 1: England* http://www.coventry.ac.uk/Global/08%20New%20Research%20Section/CWIP%20-%20BRIEFING%201%20FINAL.pdf.

Clark, T. with Heath, A. (2014) *Hard times*, New Haven, CT: Yale University Press.

Clarke, J. and Newman, J. (2014) 'States of imagination', *Soundings*, vol 57, pp 153–69.

Coie, J.D., Watt, N.F., West, S G., Hawkins, J.D., Asarnow, J.R., Markman, H.J. and Long, B. (1993) 'The science of prevention: a conceptual framework and some directions for a national research program', *American psychologist*, vol 48, no 10, pp 1013–22.

Common Cause (2010) *The case for working with our cultural values*, WWF, https://assets.wwf.org.uk/downloads/common_cause_report.pdf.

Cottam, H. (2011) 'Relational welfare', *Soundings*, vol 48, pp 134–44.

Cunha, F., Heckman, J.J. and Schennach, S.M. (2010) 'Estimating the technology of cognitive and noncognitive skill formation', *Econometrica*, vol 78, no 3, pp 883–931.

Cunliffe, V. (2015) 'Experience-sensitive epigenetic mechanisms, developmental plasticity, and the biological embedding of chronic disease risk', *WIREs Syst. Biol. Med* vol 7, pp 53–71.

Dale, P., Davies, M., Morrison, T. and Waters, J. (1986) *Dangerous families: assessment and treatment of child abuse*, London: Tavistock.

Dartington Social Research Unit, University of Warwick and Coventry University (2015) *The best start at home*, London: Early Intervention Foundation, http://www.eif.org.uk/publication/the-best-start-at-home/.

Davies, W. (2016) 'Thoughts on the sociology of Brexit', posted on 24 June, www.perc.org.uk.

Davies, W. (2017) *The limits of neoliberalism: authority, sovereignty and the logic of competition*, London: Sage.

Deneulin, S. and Stewart, F. (2002) 'Amartya Sen's contribution to development thinking', *Studies in Comparative International Development*, vol 37, no 2, pp 61–70.

Department of Health (1988) *Protecting children: a guide for social workers undertaking a comprehensive assessment*, London: HMSO.

Department of Health (1989) *The Children Act 1989: guidance and regulations, volumes 1-9*, London: HMSO.

Department of Health (1995a) *Child protection: messages from research*, London: HMSO.

Department of Health (1995b) *The challenge of partnership in child protection: practice guide*, London: HMSO.

Department of Health (2000) *Framework for the assessment of children in need and their families*, London: The Stationery Office.

DfE (2016) *Wood report: review of the role and functions of local safeguarding children boards*, London: HMSO, https://assets.publishing.service.gov.uk/government/uploads/system/uploads/attachment_data/file/526329/Alan_Wood_review.pdf.

Dillow, C. (2007) *The end of politics: New Labour and the folly of managerialism*, Petersfield: Harriman House.

Dingwall, R., Eekelaar, J. and Murray, T. (1983) *The protection of children: state intervention and family life*, Oxford: Blackwell.

Donnison, D.V. (1969) 'The Seebohm report and its implications', *International Social Work*, vol 12, no 2, pp 11–17.

Dorling, D., Gordon, D., Hillyard, P., Pantazis, C., Pemberton, S. and Tombs, S. (2008) *Criminal obsessions: why harm matters more than crime*, London: Centre for Crime and Justice Studies.

Drake, D., Simmons, K. and Smith, K. (2013) 'Building communities collaboratively: The Milton Keynes Community Mobiliser Service', *Community Development Journal*, vol 49, pp 311–26.

Durcan, G., Zlotowitz, S. and Stubbs, J. (2017) *Meeting us where we're at: Learning from INTEGRATE's work with excluded young people*, London: Centre for Mental Health, https://www.mac-uk.org/Handlers/Download.ashx?IDMF=88fa75da-8175-4b1e-a5da-8d2c6c7925a1

Eckenrode, J., Smith, E.G., McCarthy, M.E. and Dineen, M. (2014) 'Income inequality and child maltreatment in the United States', *Pediatrics*, vol 133, no 3, pp 454–61.

Edwards, A., Barnes, M., Morris, K. and Plewis, I. (2006) *The national evaluation of the Children's Fund: final report*, London: HMSO.

Edwards, R., Gillies, V. and Horsley, N. (2015) 'Brain science and early years policy: hopeful ethos or "cruel optimism"?' *Critical Social Policy*, vol 35, no 2, pp 167–87.

Evans, A. (2017) *The myth gap: what happens when arguments and evidence are not enough*, London: Transworld.

Evans K. (2016) 'Public service markets aren't working for the public good … or as markets', in Pell, C., Wilson, R. and Lowe, T. (eds) *Kittens are evil: little heresies in public policy*, Axminster: Triarchy.

Fahmy, E., Williamson, E. and Pantazis, C. (2015) *Evidence and policy review: Domestic violence and poverty, A Research Report for the Joseph Rowntree Foundation*, Bristol: University of Bristol School for Policy Studies.

Featherstone, B. (2004) *Family life and family support*, Basingstoke: Palgrave/Macmillan.

Featherstone, B. (2016) 'Telling different stories about poverty, inequality and child abuse and neglect', *Families, Relationships and Societies*, vol 5, no 1, pp 147–53.

Featherstone, B. and White, S. (2005) 'Fathers talk about their lives and services', in Ashley, C., Featherstone, B., Roskill, C., Ryan, M. and White, S. (eds) *Fathers matter*, London: Family Rights Group.

Featherstone, B., White, S. and Morris, K. (2014) *Re-imagining child protection: towards humane social work with families*, Bristol: Policy Press.

Featherstone, B., Gupta, A., Morris, K. and Warner, J. (2016) 'Let's stop feeding the risk monster: towards a social model of child protection', *Families, Relationships and Societies*, Advance Access, published on 15 February, doi.org/10.1332/204674316X14552878034622.

Featherstone, B., Gupta, A. and Mills, S. (2018) *The role of the social worker in adoption, ethics and human rights: an enquiry*, London: BASW.

Ferguson, H. (2011) *Child protection practice*, Basingstoke: Palgrave Macmillan.

Field, F. (2010) *The foundation years: preventing poor children becoming poor adults: the report of the Independent Review on Poverty and Life Chances*, HM Government, http://webarchive.nationalarchives.gov. uk/20110120090128/http://povertyreview.independent.gov.uk/ media/20254/poverty-report.pdf.

Finkelstein, V. (1980) *Attitudes and disabled people: Issues for discussion (no. 5)*, New York: World Rehabilitation Fund.

Firmin, C., Warrington, C. and Pearce, J. (2016) 'Sexual exploitation and its impact on developing sexualities and sexual relationships: the need for contextual social work interventions', *British Journal of Social Work*, vol 46, no 8, pp 2318–37.

Flood, A. (2016) 'Post-truth named word of the year by Oxford dictionaries', *The Guardian*, November 15.

Fraser, N. (2008) *Scales of justice: reimagining political space in a globalizing world*, New York, NY: Columbia University Press and Polity Press.

Friedli, L. (2009) *Mental health, resilience and inequalities*, Denmark: World Health Organization.

Frost, E. and Hoggett, P. (2008) 'Human agency and social suffering', *Critical Social Policy*, vol 28, no 4, pp 438–60.

Frost, N. and Parton, N. (2009) *Understanding children's social care: politics, policy and practice*, London: Sage.

Fuller S. (2006) *The new sociological imagination*, London: Sage.

Gilbert, N., Parton, N. and Skiveness, M. (eds) (2011) *Child protection systems: international trends and orientations*, Oxford: Oxford University Press.

Gillies, V., Edwards, R. and Horsley, N. (2017) *Challenging the politics of early intervention: who's 'saving' children and why?* Bristol: Policy Press.

Giroux, H.A. (2014) 'Totalitarian paranoia in the Post-Orwellian, surveillance state, *Cultural Studies*, vol 29, no 2, pp 108–40.

Goel, R. and Goodmark, L. (2015) *Comparative perspectives on gender violence*, Oxford: Oxford University Press.

Goffman, E. (1963) *Stigma: notes on the management of a spoiled identity*, Harmondsworth: Pelican.

Goldner, V., Penn, P., Sheinberg, M. and Walker, G. (1991) 'Love and violence: gender paradoxes in volatile attachments', *Family Process*, vol 29, no 4, pp 345–64.

Gray, M. (2009) 'Back to basics: a critique of the strengths perspective in social work', *Families in Society*, vol 92, no 1, pp 5–11.

Haebich, A. (2007) *A twilight of knowing: the Australian public and the Bringing Them Home Report*, Fitzroy, Victoria: Secretariat of National Aboriginal and Islander Child Care.

Haidt, J. (2012) *The righteous mind: why good people are divided by politics and religion*, London: Penguin.

Hall, C., Parton, N., Peckover, S. and White, S. (2010) 'Child-centric information and communication technology (ICT) and the fragmentation of child welfare practice in England', *Journal of Social Policy*, vol 39, no 3, pp 393–413.

Hasler, F. (1993) 'Developments in the disabled people's movement', in Swain, J., French, S., Barnes, C. and Thomas, C. (eds) *Disabling barriers, enabling environments*, London: Sage.

Hart, C.S. (2016) 'The school food plan and the social context of food in schools', *Cambridge Journal of Education*, vol 46, no 2, pp 211–31.

Heckman, J.J. (2013) *Giving kids a fair chance (a strategy that works)*, Boston, MA: MIT Press.

Heckman, J.J. and Masterov, D.V. (2007) 'The productivity argument for investing in young children', *Review of Agricultural Economics*, vol 29, no 3, pp 446–93.

Hochschild, A. (2002) 'Emotion management in an age of terrorism', *Soundings*, vol 20, pp 117–26.

Hoggett, P. (2009) *Politics, identity and emotion*, London: Taylor and Francis.

Holland, S., Tannock, S. and Collicott, H. (2011) 'Everybody's business? A research review of the informal safeguarding of other people's children in the UK', *Children and Society*, vol 25, no 5, pp 406–16.

Holman, R. (1983) *Resourceful friends: skills in community social work*, London: Children's Society.

Hood, R., Goldacre, A., Grant, R. and Jones, R. (2016) 'Exploring demand and provision in English Child Protection Services', *British Journal of Social Work*, vol 46, no 4, pp 923–41.

Houses of Parliament, Parliamentary Offices of Science and Technology (2013) *Epigenetics and Health*, http://researchbriefings.parliament.uk/ResearchBriefing/Summary/POST-PN-451#fullreport.

Ife, J. (2012) *Human rights and social work: towards rights-based practice* (3rd edn), Port Melbourne: Cambridge University Press.

International Society for DOHaD (2015) *The Cape Town Manifesto*, https://dohadsoc.org/wp-content/uploads/2015/11/DOHaD-Society-Manifesto-Nov-17-2015.pdf.

Ivec, M. (2013) *A necessary engagement: an international review of parent and family engagement in child protection*, Tasmania: Social Action and Research Centre, Anglicare.

Jack, G. and Gill, O. (2010) 'The role of communities in safeguarding children and young people', *Child Abuse Review*, vol 19, pp 82–96.

Jones, R. (2015) 'The end game: the marketisation and privatisation of children's social work and child protection', *Critical Social Policy*, vol 35, no 4, pp 447–69.

JTAI (2017) *The multi-agency response to children: living with domestic abuse, Prevent, protect and repair*.

Judt, T. (2011) *Ill fares the land*, London: Penguin.

Jutte, S., Bentley, H., Tallis, D., Mayes, J., Jetha, N., O'Hagan, O., Brookes, H. and McConnell, N. (2015) *How safe are our children? The most comprehensive overview of child protection in the UK*, London: NSPCC.

Kagan, J. (1998) *Three seductive ideas*, Cambridge, MA: Harvard University Press.

Kahn, F. (2010) 'Preserving human potential as freedom: a framework for regulating epigenetic harms', *Health Matrix*, vol 20, no 2, pp 259–323.

Keddell, E. (2014) 'Theorising the signs of safety approach to child protection social work: positioning, codes and power', *Children and Youth Services Review*, vol 47, pp 70–7.

Kelly, L. and Westmarland, N. (2015) *Project Mirabal evaluation of perpetrators' programmes*, https://www.dur.ac.uk/resources/criva/ProjectMirabalfinalreport.pdf.

Kimbrough-Melton, R.J. and Melton, G.B. (2015) '"Someone will notice, and someone will care": how to build strong communities for children', *Child abuse & Neglect*, vol 41, pp 67–78.

Krumer-Nevo, M. (2016) 'Poverty-aware social work', *British Journal of Social Work*, vol 46, no 6, pp 1793–808.

Krumer-Nevo, M. (2017) 'Poverty and the political: wresting the political out of and into social work theory, research and practice', *European Journal of Social Work*, vol 20, no 6, pp 811–22.

Laird, S., Morris, K.M., Archard, P. and Clawson, R. (2017a) 'Changing practice: the possibilities and limits for reshaping social work practice', *Qualitative Social Work*, doi:10.1177/1473325016688371.

Laird, S., Morris, K.M., Archard, P. and Clawson, R. (2017b) 'Working with the whole family: what case files tell us about social work practices', *Child and Family Social Work*, doi: 10.1111/cfs.12349.

Lakoff, G. (2014) *Don't think of an elephant: know your values and frame the debate* (2nd edn), Vermont: Chelsea Green Publishing.

Lakoff, G. (2017) #ProtectTheTruth, www.georgelakoff.com.

Laming, Lord (2003) *The Victoria Climbié Inquiry: report of an inquiry by Lord Laming*, London: HMSO.

Lister, R. (2004) *Poverty: key concepts*, Cambridge: Polity Press.

Lister, R. and Bennett, F. (2010) 'The new "champion of progressive ideals"', *Renewal: a Journal of Labour Politics*, vol 18, no 1/2, pp 84–109.

London Borough of Brent (1985) *A child in trust: report of the Panel of Inquiry Investigating the Circumstances Surrounding the Death of Jasmine Beckford*.

London Borough of Greenwich (1987) *A child in mind: protection of children in a responsible society: report of the Commission of Inquiry into the Circumstances Surrounding the Death of Kimberley Carlisle.*

London Borough of Lambeth (1987) *Whose child? The report of the panel appointed to inquire into the death of Tyra Henry.*

Lowe P., Lee, E. and Macvarish J. (2015) 'Growing better brains? Pregnancy and neuroscience discourses in English social and welfare policies', *Health, Risk & Society*, vol 17, no 1, pp 15–29.

MacKinnon, D. (2017) 'Regional inequality, regional policy and progressive universalism', *Soundings*, vol 65, pp 141–58.

Mansfield, B. and Guthman, J. (2014) 'Epigenetic life: biological plasticity, abnormality, and new configurations of race and reproduction', *Cultural Geographies*, vol 22, no 1, pp 3–20.

Marsh, P. and Crow, G. (1996) 'Family group conferences in child welfare services in England and Wales', in Hudson, J., Morris, A., Maxwell, G. and Galaway, B. (eds) *Family group conferences: perspectives on policy and practice*, Annandale: Federation Press.

Mason, W. (forthcoming) *Report of family reflections on helping services*, Child welfare inequalities project and University of Sheffield.

Mason, P., Ferguson, H., Morris, K. and Sen, R. (2017) *An evaluation of Leeds' Family Valued Programme*, London: DfE.

McGarvey, D. (2017) *Poverty safari: understanding the anger of Britain's underclass*, Luath Press: Edinburgh.

Megele, C. (2015) *Psychosocial and relationship-based practice*, Northwich: Critical Publishing.

Meloni, M. (2016) *Political biology: science and social values in human heredity from eugenics to epigenetics*, Basingstoke: Palgrave Macmillan.

Melton, G.B. (2010) 'It's all about relationships! The psychology of human rights', *American Journal of Orthopsychiatry*, vol 80, no 2, pp 161–9.

Mental Health Foundation (2015) *Dementia, rights and the social model of disability: A new direction for policy and practice?* https://www.mentalhealth.org.uk/publications/dementia-rights-and-social-model-disability.

Midgley, M. (2013) *Science and poetry*, London, Routledge.

Midgley, M. (2014) *Are you an illusion?* London: Routledge.

Mills, C.W. (1959) *The sociological imagination*, Oxford: Oxford University Press.

Monbiot, G. (2017) *Out of the wreckage: a new politics for an age of crisis*, London: Verso.

Montagu, A. (1972) 'Sociogenic brain damage', *American Anthropologist*, vol 74, no 5, pp 1045–61.

Morris, J. (1991) *Pride against prejudice*, London: Women's Press.

Morris, K. (2013) 'Troubled families: vulnerable families' experiences of multiple service use', *Child and Family Social Work*, vol 18, no 2, pp 198–206.

Morris, K., Barnes, M. and Mason, P. (2009) *Children, families and social exclusion: developing new understandings*, Bristol: Policy Press.

Morris, K., Marsh, P., Warwick, L. (2016) *Evaluation of Leeds FGC service: final report*, Leeds: Leeds City Council.

Morris, K., Bywaters, P. and Featherstone, B. (2017) *Time for a toxic debate?* BASW: Professional Social Work, December.

Morris, K. Mason, W., Daniel, B., Bywaters, P., Featherstone, B., Brady, G., Bunting, L. and Mirza, N. (2018a) 'Poverty, social work and child welfare interventions', *Child and Family Social Work*, doi. org/10.1111/cfs.12423.

Morris, K., Featherstone, B., Hill, K. and Ward, M. (2018b) *Stepping up, stepping down: family experiences of multiple service use*, London: FRG/Lankelly Chase.

Munro, E. (2009) 'Managing societal and institutional risk in child protection', *Risk Analysis*, vol 29, no 7, pp 1015–23.

Munro, E. (2011) *The Munro review of child protection: final report. A child centred system*, London: Department for Education.

Nadan, Y., Spilsbury, J.C. and Korbin, J.E. (2015) 'Culture and context in understanding child maltreatment: Contributions of intersectionality and neighborhood-based research', *Child Abuse and Neglect*, vol 41, pp 40–8.

New Economics Foundation (2013) *Framing the economy: the austerity story*, https://mdx.rl.talis.com/items/A34944DD-05F5-1074-8914-B5EAFD444FC9.html\.

New Economics Foundation (2015) *Fairness commissions*, www.nef. org.uk.

Nixon, J. and Humphreys, C. (2010) 'Marshalling the evidence: using intersectionality in the domestic violence frame', *Social Politics: International Studies in Gender, State and Society*, vol 17, no 2, pp 137–58.

Nussbaum, N. (2011) *Creating capabilities: the human development approach*, Cambridge, MA: Harvard University Press.

Olds, D.L., Arcoleo, K.J. and Henderson, C.R. (2010) 'Enduring effects of prenatal and infancy home visiting by nurses on maternal life course and government spending', *Archives of Paediatric Medicine*, vol 164, no 5, pp 419–24.

Oliver, M. (1983) *Social work with disabled people*, Basingstoke: Macmillan.

Oliver, M. (1990) *The politics of disablement*, Basingstoke: Macmillan.

Oliver, M. (2013) 'The social model of disability: thirty years on', *Disability & Society*, vol 28, no 7, pp 1024–6.

Oliver, M. and Barnes, C. (1998) *Disabled people and social policy: from exclusion to inclusion*, Boston, MA: Addison Wesley Longman.

O'Neill, B. (2010) 'Now the elite wants to colonise our brains' [Online] Available at: www.spiked-online.com/index.php/site/article/8499/.

ONS (2016) https://www.ons.gov.uk/peoplepopulationandcommunity/birthsdeathsandmarriages/lifeexpectancies/bulletins/lifeexpectancyatbirthandatage65bylocalareasinenglandandwales/2015-11-04#local-area-life-expectancy-at-birth.

Parton, N. (1985) *The politics of child abuse*, London: Macmillan.

Parton, N. (1991) *Governing the family: child care, child protection and the state*, Basingstoke: Palgrave Macmillan.

Parton, N. (2004) 'From Maria Colwell to Victoria Climbié: reflections on public inquiries into child abuse a generation apart', *Child Abuse Review*, vol 13, pp 80–94.

Parton, N. (2014) *The politics of child protection: contemporary developments and future directions*, Basingstoke: Palgrave Macmillan.

Pearce, J. (2013) 'A social model of "abused consent"', in Melrose, M. and Pearce, J. (eds) *Critical perspectives on child sexual exploitation and related trafficking*, Basingstoke: Palgrave Macmillan.

Pearce, W., Raman, S. and Turner, A. (2015) 'Randomised trials in context: practical problems and social aspects of evidence-based medicine and policy', *Trials*, vol 16, no 1, p 394.

Pemberton, S. (2016) *Harmful societies: understanding social harm*, Bristol: Policy Press.

Pembrey, M.E., Bygren, L.O., Kaati, G., Edvinsson, S., Northstone, K., Sjöström, M. and Golding, J., (2006) 'Sex-specific, male-line transgenerational responses in humans', *European Journal of Human Genetics*, vol 14, no 2, p 159.

Pennell, J. and Kim, M. (2010) 'Opening conversations across cultural, gender and generational divides: family and community engagement to stop violence against women and children', in Ptacek, J. (ed) *Restorative justice and violence against women*, Oxford: Oxford University Press.

Pennell, J., Rikard, R.V. and Sanders-Rice, T. (2013) 'Family violence: fathers assessing and managing their risk to children and women', *Children and Youth Services Review* vol 47, pp 36–45.

Perkins, A. (2015) *The welfare trait: how state benefits affect personality*, Basingstoke: Palgrave Macmillan.

Perry, B.D. (1997) 'Incubated in terror: neurodevelopmental factors in the "cycle of violence"', in Osofsky, J. (ed) *Children, youth and violence: the search for solutions*, New York: Guilford Press.

Peston, R. (2017) *What have we done? Why did it happen? How do we take back control?* London: Hodder and Stoughton.

Power, A. (2007) *City survivors: bringing up children in disadvantaged neighbourhoods*, Bristol: Policy Press.

Pritchard, C. and Williams, R. (2010) 'Comparing possible "child-abuse-related-deaths' in England and Wales with the major developed countries 1974–2006: signs of progress?', *British Journal of Social Work*, vol 40, pp 1700–18.

Ptacek, J. (2010) ' Resisting co-optation: three feminist challenges to anti-violence work', in Ptacek, J. (ed) *Restorative justice and violence against women*, Oxford: Oxford University Press.

Rae, A., Hamilton, R., Crisp, R. and Powell, R. (2016). *Overcoming deprivation and disconnection in UK cities*, York: Joseph Rowntree Foundation.

Reason, J. (2000) 'Human error: Models and management', *British Medical Journal*, vol 320, pp 768–70.

Richmond, Mary E. (1922) *What is social case work?* New York: Russell Sage Foundation.

Robb, M., Featherstone, B., Ruxton, M. and Ward, M. (2015) *Beyond male role models: gender identities and work with young men*, Milton Keynes: The Open University.

Robeyns, I. (2003) 'Is Nancy Fraser's critique of theories of distributive justice justified?' *Constellations*, vol 10, no 4, pp 538–54.

Robeyns, I. (2005) 'The capability approach: a theoretical survey', *Journal of Human Development*, vol 6, no 1, pp 93–117.

Roose, R., Roets, G. and Schiettecat, T. (2014) 'Implementing a strengths perspective in child welfare and protection: a challenge not to be taken lightly', *European Journal of Social Work*, vol 17, no 1, pp 3–17.

Rose, N. (2010) 'Screen and intervene: governing risky brains', *History of the Human Sciences*, vol 23, no 1, pp 79–105.

Rose, H. and Rose, S. (2012) *Genes, cells and brains: the Promethean promises of the new biology*, London: Verso.

Rothstein, M.A., Cai, Y. and Marchant, G.E. (2009) 'The ghost in our genes: legal and ethical implications of epigenetics', *Health Matrix*, vol 19, no 1, pp 1–62.

Royal College of Paediatrics and Child Health (RCPCH) (2017) *The state of child health report 2017*, https://www.rcpch.ac.uk/sites/default/files/2018-04/state_of_child_health_2017_-_full_report.pdf.

Ruch, G. (2005) 'Relationship-based practice and reflective practice: holistic approaches to contemporary child care social work', *Child and Family Social Work*, vol 10, no 2, pp 111–23.

Ruch, G., Turney, D. and Ward, A. (2010) *Relationship-based social work: getting to the heart of practice*. London: Jessica Kingsley Publishers.

Saar-Heiman, Y., Lavie-Ajayi, M. and Krumer-Nevo, M. (2017) 'Poverty-aware social work practice: service users' perspectives', *Child and Family Social Work*, vol 22, no 2, pp 1054–63.

Sayer, A. (2017) 'Responding to the Troubled Families Programme: framing the injuries of inequality', *Social Policy and Society*, vol 16, no 1, pp 155–64.

Scrambler, G. (2018) *Weaponising stigma*, http://www.grahamscambler. com/weaponising-stigma/.

Seddon, J. (2008) *Systems thinking in the public sector: the failure of the reform regime ... and a manifesto for a better way*, Devon: Triarchy Press.

Seebohm Report (1968) *Report of the Committee on Local Authority and Allied Personal Social Services*, London: HMSO.

Sen, A. (2009) *The idea of justice*, London, Allen Lane.

Sen, R., Morris, K., Burford, G., Featherstone, B. and Webb, C. (2018) '"When you're sitting in the room with two people one of whom... has bashed the hell out of the other": Possibilities and challenges in the use of FGCs and restorative practice following domestic violence', *Children and Youth Services Review*, doi: 10.1016/j. childyouth.2018.03.027.

Shakespeare, T. and Watson, N. (2002) 'The social model of disability: an outdated ideology?' *Research in Social Science and Disability*, vol 2, pp 9–28.

Shaw, I., Bell, M., Sinclair, I., Sloper, P., Mitchell, W., Dyson, P., Clayden, J. and Rafferty, J. (2009) 'An exemplary scheme? An evaluation of the integrated children's system', *British Journal of Social Work*, vol 39, no 4, pp 613–26.

Shonkoff, J.P. and Bales, S. (2011) 'Science does not speak for itself: translating child development research for the public and its policymakers', *Child Development*, vol 82, no 1, pp 17–32.

Smith, M.L. and Seward, C. (2009) 'The relational ontology of Amartya Sen's capability approach: incorporating social and individual causes', *Journal of Human Development and Capabilities*, vol 10, no 2, pp 213–35.

Sokoloff, N. and Dupont, I. (2005) 'Domestic violence at the intersections of race, class, and gender', *Violence Against Women*, vol 11, no 1, pp 38–64.

Solnit, R. (2016) *Hope in the dark: untold histories, wild possibilities*, London: Cannongate.

Solnit, R. (2017) *The mother of all questions: further feminisms*, London: Granta.

Stanley, N. and Humphreys, C. (2017) 'Identifying the key components of a "whole family" intervention for families experiencing domestic violence and abuse', *Journal of Gender-Based Violence*, vol 1, no 1, pp 99–115.

Stevenson, L. (2016) 'Ofsted gives first outstanding grades for children's services to two London councils', *Community Care*, March, 29.

Terzi, L. (2004) 'The social model of disability: a philosophical critique', *Journal of Applied philosophy*, vol 21, no 2, pp 141–57.

The Care Inquiry – *Making not Breaking: Building relationships for out most vulnerable children* is available at: http://www.frg.org.uk/images/Policy_Papers/care-inquiry-full-report-april-2013.pdf

Thomas, C. (1999) *Female forms: experiencing and understanding disability*, Buckingham: Open University Press.

Thomas, C. (2004) 'How is disability understood? An examination of sociological approaches', *Disability & Society*, vol 19, no 6, pp 569–83.

Thomas, C. and Milligan, C. (2015). *How can and should UK society adjust to dementia?*, York: Joseph Rowntree Foundation.

Thompson, S. and Hoggett, P. (2012) (eds) *Politics and the emotions, the affective turn in contemporary political studies*, London: Bloomsbury Publishing.

Thorpe, D. (1994) *Evaluating child protection*, Buckingham: Open University Press.

Tobis, D. (2013) *From pariahs to partners: how parents and their allies changed New York City's child welfare system*, Oxford: Oxford University Press.

Tuc, V. (2012) 'Resistant parents and child protection: knowledge Base, pointers for practice and implications for policy', *Child Abuse Review*, vol 12, no 1, pp 5–19.

Tunstill, J. and Blewett, J. (2015) 'Mapping the journey: outcome-focused practice and the role of interim outcomes in family support services', *Child & Family Social Work*, vol 20, no, 2 pp 234–43.

Turnell, A. and Edwards, S. (1999) *Signs of safety: a solution and safety oriented approach to child protection casework*, New York: Norton.

UNDP (1990) *Human Development Report 1990: concept and measurement of human development*, New York: Oxford University Press.

Valentine, C.A., Valentine, B., Aptheker, H., Berreman, G.D., Genovés, S., Henderson, N.B., Hoffman, M.J., Jaquith, J.R., Jerison, H.J., Lewis, D.K., Montagu, A., Panoff, M., Remy, A. and Seltzer, M.R. (1975) 'Brain damage and the intellectual defense of inequality [and comments and reply]' *Current Anthropology*, vol 6, no 1, pp 117–50.

Vernon, A. (1996) 'A stranger in many camps: the experience of disabled black and ethnic minority women', in Morris, J. (ed) *Encounters with strangers: feminism and disability*, London: Womens Press, pp 48–67.

Viner, R.M., Hargreaves, D.S., Coffey, C., Patton, G.C. and Wolfe, I. (2014) 'Deaths in young people aged 0–24 years in the UK compared with the EU15+ countries, 1970–2008: analysis of the WHO Mortality Database', *The Lancet*, vol 384, no 9946, pp 880–92.

Wacquant L. (2010) 'Crafting the neoliberal state: Workfare, Prisonfare, and social insecurity', *Sociological Forum*, vol 25, no 2, pp 197–220.

Walkerdine, V. and Lucey, H. (1989) *Democracy in the kitchen*, London: Virago.

Warner, J. (2015) *The emotional politics of social work and child protection*, Bristol: Policy Press.

Wastell, D. (2011), *Managers as designers in the public services: beyond technomagic*, Devon: Triarchy Press.

Wastell, D. and White, S. (2012) 'Blinded by neuroscience: social policy and the infant brain', *Families Relationships and Societies: An International Journal of Research and Debate*, vol 1, no 3, pp 397–414.

Wastell D. and White, S. (2017) *Blinded by science: social implications of epigenetics and neuroscience*, Bristol: Policy Press.

Webb, C.J. and Bywaters, P. (2018) 'Austerity, rationing and inequity: trends in children's and young peoples' services expenditure in England between 2010 and 2015', *Local Government Studies*, Advance access, published 6 February 2018, DOI: 10.1080/03003930.2018.1430028.

Weinberg, M. (2009) 'Moral distress', *Canadian Social Work Review*, vol 26, no 2, pp 139–51.

Weinberg, M. and Campbell, C. (2014) 'From codes to contextual collaborations: shifting the thinking about ethics in social work', *Journal of Progressive Human Services*, vol 49, pp 25–37.

Weiss-Gal, I. and Savaya, R. (2012) 'Teaching policy practice: a hands-on seminar for social workers in Israel', *Journal of Policy Practice*, vol 11, no 3, pp 139–57

White, S. (1998) 'Interdiscursivity and child welfare: the ascent and durability of psycho-legalism', *The Sociological Review* vol 46, no 2, pp 264–92.

White, S., Wastell, D., Broadhurst, K. and Hall, C. (2010) 'When policy o'erleaps itself: the "tragic tale" of the integrated children's system', *Critical Social Policy*, vol 30, no 3, pp 405–29.

White, S., Wastell, D., Smith, S., Hall, C., Whitaker, E., Debelle, G., Mannion, R. and Waring, J. (2015) 'Improving practice in safeguarding at the interface between hospital services and children's social care: a mixed-methods case study', Health Services and Delivery Research, vol 3, no 4, https://www.journalslibrary.nihr.ac.uk/hsdr/hsdr03040/#/full-report.

Wilkinson, R. and Pickett, K. (2009) The spirit level: why more equal societies always do better, London: Penguin.

Williams, C. and Briskman, L. (2015) 'Reviving social work through moral outrage', Critical and Radical Social Work, vol 3, no 1, pp 3–17.

Williams, S. (2017) 'Redrawing the line: how lay people construct neglect', Child Abuse and Neglect, vol 68, pp 11–24.

Wolfe, I., Macfarlane, A., Donkin, A., Marmot, M. and Viner, R. (2014) Why children die: death in infants, children, and young people in the UK—Part A. London: Royal College of Paediatrics and Child Health and National Children's Bureau.

Young, A.F. and Ashton, A.F. (1956) British social work in the nineteenth century, London: Routledge and Kegan Paul.

Index